# *Spotlight*
## ON FIRST CERTIFICATE

An integrated course for the
First Certificate Examination

CASSELL

Cassell Publishers Limited
Villiers House
41–47 Strand
London WC2N 5JE



First published 1990
Reprinted 1991

British Library Cataloguing in Publication Data
Digby, Christine
Spotlight on First Certificate.
Students' book
1. English language – for schools
I. Title II. Myers, John III. Pitkeathly, Iain
428

ISBN 0–304–31888–4
Teacher's Book 0–304–31891–4
Cassettes (2) 0–304–31889–2

Design by Barrie Richardson
Illustrations by Peter Smith, Barrie Richardson and Tony Richardson
Typesetting by Fakenham Photosetting Limited, Fakenham, Norfolk
Printed and bound in Great Britain by the Bath Press, Avon.

The authors and Publishers would like to thank the following for permission to use their copyright material:

'Who buys designer clothes?' p. 10 from 'The Fashion Conspiracy', by Nicholas Coleridge and 'My Cousin Rachel' (adapted) p. 34 reprinted by permission of William Heinemann Ltd, Publishers; 'Not just a pretty face', p. 13, 'Interview with a star', p. 96; 'Richard Branson the Virgin man', p. 46, Paul Mansfield; 'The Chinese Art of Geomancy', p. 39, reference from 'The Atlas of Mysterious Places', published by Weidenfeld and Nicolson © Marshall Editions Ltd; Ski clothing, p. 65, EP Publishing Ltd; 'Tonight at Noon', p. 76 Adrian Henri; 'First Aid', p. 86, The Consumers Association; Advertisements, p. 108/109, The Sunday Times; 'Six men in a bath', p. 118, The Independent; 'Heroic Failures', p. 126 from 'The Return of Heroic Failures', Secker and Warburg.

Photographs by kind permission of:

Thompson holidays, p. 9; Dennis Mansell, p. 9; Norman Hartnell, p. 10; Clare Park, p. 13; Candice Temple, p. 22, p. 51, p. 116; The Times Picture Library, p. 17, p. 38, p. 119; Alaska division of Tourism, p. 29; Stephen Gibson, Tom Kidd, The Sunday Times, p. 31; Thames TV, p. 38; Frederick Warne and Company, p. 38; Mary Evans Picture Library, p. 38, p. 39; Robert Harding, p. 38; Science Museum Library, p. 40; Barnaby's Picture Library, p. 43; Aerofilms, p. 43; Virgin Group Ltd, p. 46, p. 47; Richard and Sally Greenhill, p. 67; Stuart Napier, p. 71; David Redfern, p. 75; B T Batsford Ltd, p. 77; Columbia Tristar, p. 96; Kobal Collection, p. 98; Ian Parry, p. 123; Orpix, inside back cover.

While every effort has been made to trace copyright owners, the Publishers would be pleased to hear from any other parties who feel they hold rights to any of the material that has been included.

The authors, Christine Digby, John Myers and Iain Pitkeathly, were staff members of the inlingua School of Languages, Brighton.

# *Contents*

# Introduction

This book is specifically designed for students preparing for the First Certificate in English Examination. It offers approximately 120–140 hours of classroom teaching with a self-access section allowing further study at home.

It is a multi-syllabus based coursebook that aims to give students a thorough grounding in the grammatical forms, lexical items and phonological points needed to pass the FCE exam as well as practice in the four skills of reading, writing, listening and speaking. It also introduces students to the format and 'feel' of the exam by gradually introducing 'exam type' questions through a variety of activities organised into topic-based units that aim to stimulate learners by dealing with subjects that appeal to their interest and imagination. Two special features of the book are the review of the grammatical points and the Examination 'advice blocks' which appear throughout the book.

The section called 'Spotlight on Language' is a review of the most important grammatical points from each unit, with exercises which may be used by the student for self study, as the answers to these exercises, unlike those in the rest of the students' book, are to be found within the section. The Examination 'advice blocks' give students advice on what each paper demands and how to plan the answers.

The book is divided into 13 units, with an Introductory unit which explains exactly what is in each paper and which gives typical examples. At regular intervals throughout the book there are Progress Tests and at the end, a Mock Examination modelled on the First Certificate Examination, allowing teachers to test without having to search for other material.

The book comes with a detailed Teacher's Book containing a key to the exercises, tapescripts and also advice on methodology, examination hints, summaries of the points contained in each unit and suggested extra activities. There are two C-60 cassettes.

# Introductory Unit

The Cambridge First Certificate Examinations are held twice a year, in the middle of June and the middle of December. This unit explains the examination and how this book helps you in your examination preparation.

There are also examples from the five papers in the exam which are provided solely as examples, not as exercises to be answered.

## Paper 1: Reading comprehension

This is a one-hour paper and consists entirely of multiple-choice questions. Section A has 25 questions based on grammar points and vocabulary items set in the context of sentences. Look at this example:

The police were .......... everybody's bags for dangerous weapons.
A looking B controlling C checking D testing

Answer: C

You have to decide which one of the four alternatives is correct and enter your choice on the answer paper.

Section B consists of 15 multiple-choice questions which test your understanding of the meaning and content of three or more texts. The texts are usually extracts from novels and advertisements or sets of instructions. Look at this example:

My father did not like me. My presence was insistently physical. He was a fastidious man. He dusted the chair on which the cat had been lying before occupying it himself. He ate a banana with a knife and fork – to modern minds a dead give-away if ever there was one. In later years I had to supply various subsidiary kinds of fuel for the furnaces of his hatred. In infancy my existence was enough.

The author's father did not like him because

A he was untidy.
B he was deliberately naughty.
C he made too much noise.
D his presence annoyed him.

Again you have to decide which is the best answer.
Answer: D

The 25 questions in Section A are worth 1 mark each and the 15 questions in Section B 2 marks each, giving a total of 55 marks for the paper, which is scaled down to 40.

## Paper 2: Composition

In this paper you have to write two compositions in an hour and a half. You choose from five questions (including the set book question) the two that you feel you can do best. The choice usually includes a letter, a descriptive piece, a narrative, a discursive piece and a question based on a set book that you may have chosen to do. Note here that you do not have to do a set book, but if you do, that the books change every year. Your examination secretary or school should be able to give you more information about this, as this book does not deal with the set books option.

You must write the compositions in between 120 and 180 words.

Here are some example titles:

### Letter

You have been staying with a friend. Write a letter to your friend thanking him or her for letting you stay and describing your journey home.

### Descriptive

Describe a famous tourist attraction in your country.

### Narrative

You are staying on the top floor of a large hotel and the fire alarm goes off. Describe what happens next.

### Discursive

The town or the country? Which is better to live in?

Each composition is worth 20 marks, giving a total of 40 marks for the paper.

## Paper 3: Use of English

This is a two-hour paper containing a variety of different questions which test your grammar, vocabulary and control of language. The following are examples of the types of questions in this paper:

### Gap Filling

You are given a text from which 20 words have been removed. You have to try and think what the missing words are, using the context of the text and your own knowledge of grammar. It is useful to try to think first about what part of speech the word is likely to be, ie noun, adjective, verb etc, and then try to identify the correct word. Look at this example:

I often went to the seaside when I was a child. I loved watching fishermen landing their …… (1) and seeing the gulls circling …… (2). Now …… (3) seems such …… (4) long time ago.

Answers: 1 nets 2 above 3 it 4 a

### Sentence Transformation

You are given ten pairs of sentences. The first sentence in each pair is written in full but for the second sentence you are only given the first few words. You have to complete the sentence so that it has exactly the same meaning as the first sentence. Look at these examples:

**a** He's much taller than his brother.

His brother ..........................................

**b** They are filming another programme here next week.

Another programme .............................

**c** Don't forget to bring your swimming costume.

He told me .........................................

Answers: **a** His brother is much shorter than him.
**b** Another programme will be filmed here next week.
**c** He told me not to forget to bring my swimming costume.

### Word Building

You are given a set of questions consisting of a sentence with a word missing and a word that you have to put in the gap by changing it into another part of speech, eg from a noun to an adverb. Look at these examples:

**a** Thank you for a ......... party. (WONDER)

**b** I had a very happy .......... when I was young. (CHILD)

**c** He is totally ..........; he can never find things. (ORGANISE)

Answers: **a** wonderful **b** childhood **c** disorganised

### Dialogue Completion

You are given a dialogue which is incomplete and have to fill in the missing parts with expressions which not only are correct in terms of grammar but which also make sense of the conversation. Look at this example:

A: Good morning. Can I help you?

B: (1) ................................................?

A: Yes, toys are on the second floor.

B: Is there (2) .......................................?

A: Yes, the lift is just over there on the right.

B: Oh! Another question (3) ....................?

A: If you have a banker's card to support your cheque.

Answers: **1** Have you got/Do you have a toy department?
**2** Is there a lift?
**3** Can I pay by cheque?

### Expanded Texts

You are given a text where the key words are included but some other words are missing. You have to put in the additional words and also make any changes of tense, etc, which are necessary to produce good English. Look at this example:

Dear Margaret,

I/very pleased/receive/your letter/morning.

a) ..................................................

I/love/come/visit/but/unfortunately/I/holiday/ that time.

b) ..................................................

Would/possible/be/come/week/later?

c) ..................................................

Answers: **a** I was very pleased to receive your letter this morning.
**b** I would love to come and visit you but unfortunately I'll be on holiday at that time.
**c** Would it be possible to come a week later?

## Paragraph Writing

Here you are given textual or graphical information and you have to summarise it or represent it. An example would be that you were given a description of three people and three different holiday destinations and you are asked to write a suggestion of the most suitable holiday destinations for them with your reasons for the suggestions.

## Other Exercises

In this paper there are a variety of different exercises used, eg opposites, superlatives, phrasal verbs etc. You will see a wide range of them covered in this book. This paper is worth 40 marks.

# Paper 4: Listening comprehension

This paper tests your understanding of spoken English from a tape. The type of questions vary from year to year. Now listen to the cassette and try to complete the answers.

## First Part

Put a tick against the two houses Paul describes:

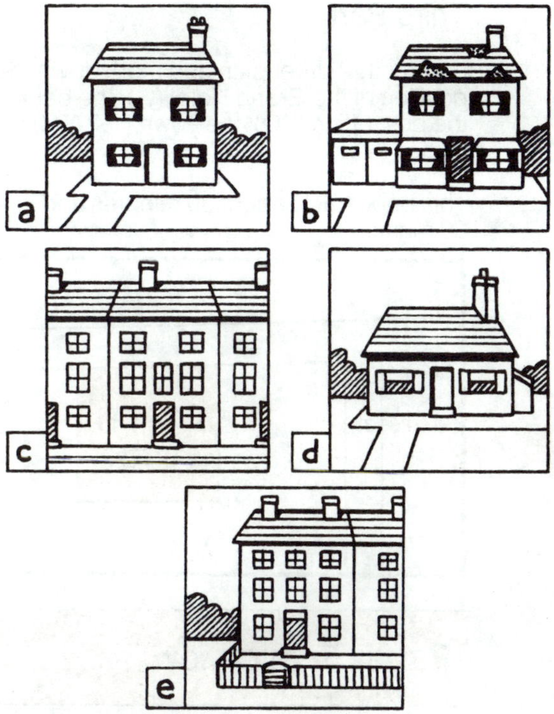


Answer: **b** and **e**

## Second Part

Fill in the information missing from this form.

Holiday destination ............................ (1)

Flight number .................................... (2)

Hotel .............................................. (3)

Departure date ................................. (4)

Number of people in party .................... (5)

Answers: **1** Rome
**2** BA 1933
**3** Concorde
**4** 18th October
**5** 4

## Third Part

Look at this street plan and mark down the position of the Grand Hotel (G), the bank (B), the post office (PO), the Town Hall (TH) and the station (S).

This paper lasts about 30 minutes and is worth 20 marks.

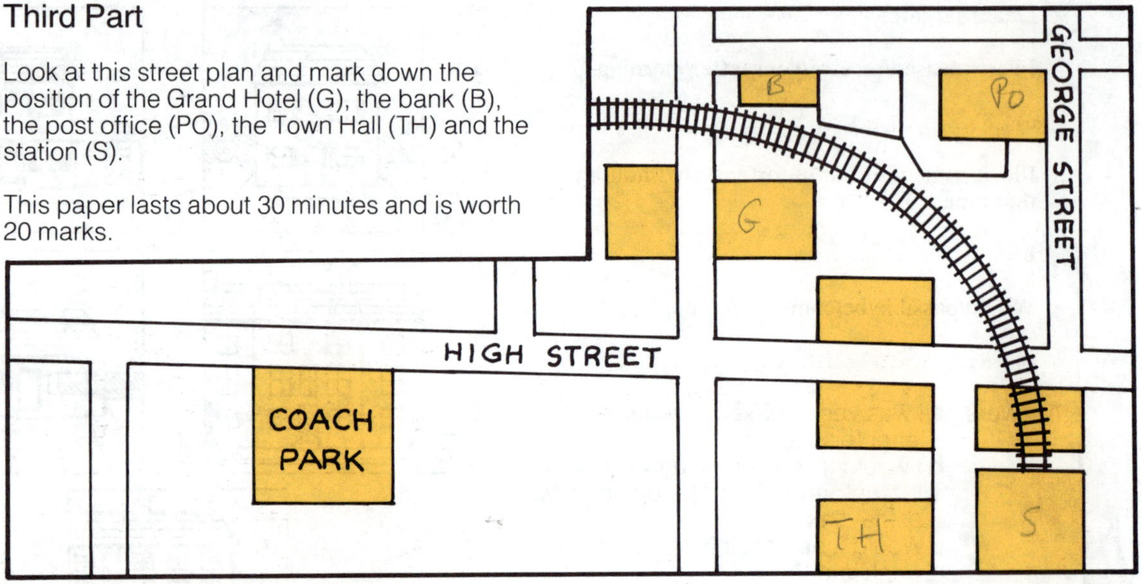


## Paper 5: Interview

This paper tests your ability to speak English. You will take part in a conversation with an examiner either by yourself or with a group of other students. The conversation will be based on a topic. For example: 'Travel', 'Food' or 'Studies'. Each interview is different but it usually follows the pattern described here.

*Menu*

At the start of the interview you will be asked to talk about or describe one or more photographs which the examiner will give you. You may then be asked to look at a written passage and give your views on it. It may be an advertisement, brochure, leaflet etc. This may then be followed by a communicative activity with the examiner and maybe other students.

Note: If you have studied a set book you may choose to discuss this at the interview.

Now look at the two photographs and the hotel descriptions opposite and the menu on this page and then listen to a student being interviewed.

This paper is worth 40 marks.

## How many marks are needed to pass?

There are five grades awarded by Cambridge: A, B, C, D and E, A, B and C are pass grades, with A being the highest. D and E are both fail grades. The examination as a whole is marked out of 180 and to pass, candidates will need a total of around 100. It is not possible to state exactly how many marks are allotted to each paper as there is some balancing done at the end. But if you are achieving about 60% on your Progress Tests, then you should have the required level of English to pass.

*Photograph 1*

*Photograph 2*

*Hotel Descriptions*

**HOTEL VICTORIA**

**Position:** Situated in the heart of Ladar, the large and lively Victoria is about 20 minutes' walk from the beach, with a wide range of shops, restaurants and nightlife close by.
**Amenities:** Large swimming pool ● Extensive gardens ● Sun terraces ● Large restaurant ● Lounge ● Bar ● TV room ● Hairdressers ● Range of shops ● Free hourly bus service to the beach ● Hotel accepts Visa, Access, American Express and Diners Club credit cards.
**Meals:** All meals are buffet service.
**Entertainment:** Full entertainment programme and live music most nights.
**Sports:** 2 tennis courts ● Table tennis ● Water sports available on beach.
**Bedrooms:** All twins have bath, loo, balcony ● All singles have bath, loo, balcony.
**Our opinion:** If you are looking for a lively holiday atmosphere with plenty to do in the heart of Ladar, the Victoria offers a good value for money choice.

**ROYAL APARTMENTS**

**SLEEPS 1–3 PEOPLE**

**Position:** This well equipped apartment block has a sunny hillside position and is a 10 minute downhill walk to the beach, shops and bars of this popular resort.
**Apartments:** Every apartment has one bedroom ● lounge with convertible sofa ● kitchenette with 2 electric rings and fridge ● bathroom with bath and shower ● maid service 6 days a week ● linen changed twice weekly.
**Amenities:** Large pool ● Sunbathing area with water chute ● Pool bar ● Supermarket ● Gift shop ● Restaurant ● Apartments accept American Express, Visa, Access and Diners Club credit cards.
**Entertainment:** Nightly dancing to live band.
**Our opinion:** Good views over Ladar make this one of the most attractive apartment complexes in the resort.

UNIT 1

# Fashion

## Reading: Designer clothes

### Who buys designer clothes?

The champagne is flowing and the music is playing. Cameras are flashing and the audience is clapping. Some of them are busy writing notes. It is a fashion show where the latest collection by a well-known designer is being exhibited for the first time. The beautiful models are wearing outfits which are probably as expensive as an average car.

Newspaper articles on the clothes are being prepared by the 700 or more journalists present which will be read by millions of people all over the world. It is a time for business as well as glamour. The number of actual customers is very small yet the deals involve large sums of money.

In fact not many people realise just how rich and powerful the people who design these clothes have become. It shocks the designers themselves that a company such as Pierre Cardin for example has an annual turnover of around $2.5 billion, which is more than the output of each of the eight poorest nations in the world.

Fashion designers are no longer merely dressmakers. They have become world leaders of taste and style and have acquired the symbols of success which were previously owned by only their richest customers. Outside their luxury houses are expensive cars; inside, the walls are covered with priceless works of art, and the rooms are filled with pieces of antique furniture.

A fashion designer has to work extremely hard to reach the top of his profession and stay there, though. Many work seven days a week to produce 500 designs for each collection. In one year they can design over three thousand outfits.

Who buys these clothes? They are certainly not for the High Street. Many of the customers are the wives of successful American businessmen. While their husbands are making deals on Wall Street they are spending millions at fashion shows in Paris and Tokyo. Just as their husbands are important members of the business world, they too play an important role in the fashion world. The women's social calendar is as full as the men's business diary and their financial power is impressive too. Each of them spends an average of $350,000 a year on their wardrobe.

What's more, these extravagant clothes are only worn once. This is normally at one of the many charity events which are arranged by these women to raise money for worthy causes. Perhaps when they organise these events they feel better about spending so much money on their appearance. Indeed these events raise vast sums of money. In 1987, the 800 charity balls held in the USA raised over $400 million. Besides, the women also want to be noticed. When they attend these functions they are certain to get their photographs in the glossy fashion magazines and their names in the gossip columns.

Most ordinary people who see the collections of high-fashion clothes in the newspapers or on TV laugh at the outrageous designs and wonder who wears such ridiculous outfits. However, although most people cannot afford these outfits, the world is definitely becoming more fashion conscious. The designers are beginning to appear in the High Street with clothes for the ordinary shopper.

## Advice on Reading Comprehension (Paper 1 Section B)

1. Always read the text through from start to finish BEFORE looking at the questions.
2. Read the questions WITHOUT looking at the four possible answers and try to answer in your own words first from the information in the text.

It may help to change statements into questions, eg Are the clothes at the fashion show ......? – What do you know about them? Now look at the four answers and choose the best one. Remember that three of the alternatives are WRONG – start by eliminating the most obviously wrong.

**1** The clothes at the fashion show are
- **a** very expensive.
- **b** never going to be worn again.
- **c** bought by millions of customers.
- **d** designed for wearing in a car.

**2** Fashion designers
- **a** sell clothes to the poorest countries.
- **b** earn over $2 billion a year.
- **c** have a lot of influence.
- **d** produce 500 designs a week.

**3** When do their customers wear the clothes?
- **a** at fashion shows in Paris and Tokyo.
- **b** every day.
- **c** at fund raising occasions.
- **d** at business meetings.

## Word search

Find words in the text that mean the same as:

**1** shown in public

**2** people employed to show clothes to buyers

**3** sets of clothes to be worn together

**4** agreement/arrangements in business

**5** of great value/too valuable to say

**6** paying out money for what you want

## **Writing:** Link words of connection

Link words like these are used to link sentences of similar meaning or argument. This is useful when we want to continue talking about a topic or add some more information.

| and / as well as / besides / what's more / also / too |
|---|

Using the words or phrases in the box link the sentences below: there is more than one possible answer. Use each of the words or phrases at least once. An example has been done for you:

I like Cardin clothes.
I often wear his perfume.

Answer: As well as buying Cardin clothes, I often wear his perfume.

**1** Fred works as a designer.
Fred helps organise fashion shows.

**2** Jill is wearing a woollen dress.
Jill is wearing brown leather boots.

**3** More people are buying fashion magazines.
There are more customers for designer clothes.

**4** Fashion is a very important industry.
Designer clothes are appearing in the High Street.

**5** That coat is too large for you.
You can't afford it.

**6** A fashion show is a glamorous event.
Many business deals are made.

## **Communication activity:** Questionnaire

### Are you a sheep or a goat?

Find out how fashion conscious you are in our exciting new quiz! Find your fashion rating by choosing answer a, b or c, whichever is nearest to the truth.

Ask your partner:

**1** How often do you wear formal clothes

A at work?

a always b often c rarely

B in a restaurant?

a sometimes b occasionally
c always

C at a formal occasion?

a often b sometimes c always

D at the weekend?

a often b rarely c never

**2** How often do you buy new clothes

A for work?

a once a week b once a month
c when I feel like it

B for leisure?

a once a week b once a year
c once a month

**3** How often do you go window shopping?

a occasionally b never c often

**4** How often do you buy new shoes

A for sport?

a rarely b often c very rarely

B for work?

a often b very rarely
c occasionally

C for casual wear?

a never b often c rarely

**5** How often do you read fashion magazines?

a often b rarely c never

**6** How often do you change your hairstyle?

a often b sometimes c never

**7** How often do you throw away old clothes?

a often b sometimes c never

**8** How often do you notice what other people are wearing?

a always b sometimes c rarely

**9** How often do you copy what other people are wearing?

a never b not often c often

**10** How often do you ask for other people's opinion?

a rarely b never c often

To calculate your score turn to page 17 to find out how many points to give each answer.

# **Listening:** Not just a pretty face

**Paul Mansfield interviews Clare Park.**

> **Advice on Listening Comprehension Multiple-Choice Questions (Paper 4)**
>
> You are allowed to hear the passages twice in the examination but unlike Paper 1 (Section B) you cannot see the text. Therefore use the preparation time before the first listening to make sure a) you understand the questions and b) you have some idea what the passage is about (ie try to predict the topic from the introduction and the questions).

Choose the answer which best completes the sentences.

**1** Clare Park
- **a** sent her photograph to Vogue.
- **b** won a dance competition in 1976.
- **c** was originally a ballet dancer.
- **d** injured her leg.

**2** Most models
- **a** only work in their holidays.
- **b** are much younger nowadays.
- **c** aren't interested in other people.
- **d** stay a long time in the profession.

**3** Clare
- **a** thinks colour film is easier to use.
- **b** takes most photographs of men.
- **c** thinks it is important to make her subjects relax.
- **d** doesn't model any more.

**4** Clare
- **a** is a photographer's assistant.
- **b** works for a photographic magazine.
- **c** has her own business.
- **d** only takes photographs occasionally.

**5** Clare's previous experience
- **a** is an advantage in her new career.
- **b** is a disadvantage in her new career.
- **c** makes her more relaxed.
- **d** is not relevant.

**6** As an agent, Clare
- **a** looks at new photographs.
- **b** sends advice to magazines.
- **c** is well-known.
- **d** teaches photography.

## **Interview Practice:** Describing people

**Vocabulary**

Put these words into three categories – clothes, jewellery, and accessories.

jacket, shirt, coat, handbag, skirt, tie, earring, belt, gloves, shoes, socks, jeans, dress, suit, boots, sandals, necklace, trousers, bracelet, T-shirt, ring, pullover, sweater, trainers, scarf, briefcase, hat, pyjamas, stockings, swimming costume.

What is this man
- a holding?
- b carrying?
- c wearing?

## **Listening:** Buying clothes

### Exercise 1

Listen to these dialogues and write down the expressions used in the following situations:

**1** You don't need the assistant at the moment. ..............................................................................

**2** You want the assistant's attention. ..............................................................................

**3** Your item of clothing is the wrong size. ..............................................................................

**4** You decide to buy something. ..............................................................................

**5** You are not ready to buy anything. ..............................................................................

### Exercise 2

Listen again to the dialogues. You will hear three multi-word verbs that can be used to complete the following sentences:
One woman wants to know if the skirt is her size, so she goes into the changing room to (1) ......... .............. it. ...............

Another customer wants a coat. Because it is tight, she (2) ............... her pullover ................... and (3) .............. the coat ............... over her shirt, and it fits perfectly.

## **Reading:** Fashion matters

**BBC 9.30**

Jackie Lewis is sent to Friland to investigate how an unscrupulous clothes company is making a fortune out of other people's designs. She traces how the designs are stolen at the Paris fashion shows and then smuggled out by plane to a secret location in Friland. There they are made up into dress patterns. Then they are put together by young girls in remote villages. When the dresses are finished they are sent back to Europe and are put on show in your local High Street shop.

We see the clothes as they are being sewn together in one of the village workshops and one of the families is interviewed about the work they do and the wages they receive. Finally we follow the clothes back to England and see them as they are put in the window in a well-known High Street store.

Look at this diagram and fill in the spaces using the information from the text above.

**A** The .............. are stolen at the Paris fashion shows.

**B** They are smuggled out .............. plane.

**C** The designs are .............. to Friland.

**D** They .............. made up into dress patterns.

**E** They are sewn together by ..................

**F** They are .............. .............. Europe.

**G** They are .............. .............. in the window in the High St store.

## **Listening:** Answer-phone message

### Advice on Listening Comprehension completion exercises

Before you hear the text you are given some short information about the passage and a few moments to look at the form or table to be completed. Use this opportunity to predict what the missing items are. For example, in this exercise you have to listen for different types of numbers, eg telephone numbers etc.

Listen to this message left on a company's answer-phone and complete the order form below. (Some of the information has been filled in for you.)

**BINGLESWORTH TRADING COMPANY – CLOTHING WHOLESALER**
18 Watery Lane, Ashford, Kent, AH3 4CT
Telephone (0233) 234456 Telex – BT 9870B

ORDER FORM

| Name of company: | Address: | Tel. No: |
|---|---|---|
| Amanda Clothing Company | The High Street Hothfield | (1) 876 244 |

Name of contact:
Tim Wilson

| ITEMS | ORDER NO. | COLOURS | QUANTITY | TOTAL |
|---|---|---|---|---|
| Skirts | (2) PJ 778 | wt | 50 | 50 |
| Trousers | (3) S1920 | gn<br>bk<br>wt | (4) 0<br>(5) 30<br>(6) 30 | 60 |
| Jackets | TE783 | b<br>bl<br>gn | (7) 5<br>(8) 5<br>(9) 5 | |

Colour code: wt = white, bk = black, bl = blue, gn = green, b = beige

## **Use of English:** Weddings

Read the following passage and complete the dialogue below.

In England most people have a civil wedding but a large number get married in a church. A wedding is always a special occasion wherever you choose to celebrate it, but a church wedding is often more fun as there are more traditions connected with it. For the wedding ceremony itself the bride usually wears a white dress and traditionally something old, something new, something borrowed, something blue. She also carries a bouquet of flowers which she throws to the guests when she leaves the church. The groom sometimes wears a top hat and tails; everyone else wears their smartest clothes. After the ceremony everyone goes outside the church and throws confetti or rice at the newly married couple while the photographer takes the wedding portrait, and then they go to the wedding reception. At the reception various members of the family and guests make speeches. After the party is over the bride and groom go on their honeymoon.

### Exercise

A is asking about English weddings. Write out A's questions in full to complete the dialogue.

**1** A: Where/most people/get married?

..................................................................

B: In a Registry Office.

**2** A: How many people/get married/church?

..................................................................

B: Well, a large number do.

**3** A: Who/wear/white dress?

..................................................................

B: The bride does.

**4** A: What/groom/wear?

..................................................................

B: He sometimes wears a top hat and tails.

**5** A: What/guest/throw/after the ceremony?

..................................................................

B: Confetti or rice.

**6** A: Who/throw/bouquet?

..................................................................

B: The bride.

**7** A: What/everybody/do/after the ceremony?

..................................................................

B: They go to the reception.

**8** A: Who/make/speeches?

..................................................................

B: Some of the guests and members of the family.

**9** A: What/happen/after the reception?

..................................................................

B: The husband and wife go on honeymoon and live happily ever after!

## Writing: A Festival

### Advice on writing descriptive compositions (Paper 2)

Underline the important words in the title and then remember only to write about the subject in question.
Write between 120 and 180 words only.

**1** Describe a typical ceremony or festival in your country.

**2** A family celebration is being planned. Describe the preparations being made and the arrangements.

Think about the different customs and traditions connected with the event. What do people usually do? Why? Do they wear special clothes, prepare special food, play special music? Use some of the following link words to help you:

First of all
Then .........
Next .........
After that .........
Finally .........

**Are you a sheep or a goat? from p. 12**

**Scores**

| | | a | b | c |
|---|---|---|---|---|
| **1** | A | 1 | 2 | 3 |
| | B | 2 | 3 | 1 |
| | C | 2 | 3 | 1 |
| | D | 1 | 2 | 3 |
| **2** | A | 2 | 1 | 3 |
| | B | 3 | 1 | 2 |
| **3** | | 3 | 1 | 2 |
| **4** | A | 3 | 2 | 1 |
| | B | 1 | 3 | 2 |
| | C | 1 | 2 | 3 |

| | a | b | c |
|---|---|---|---|
| **5** | 2 | 3 | 1 |
| **6** | 1 | 2 | 3 |
| **7** | 2 | 3 | 1 |
| **8** | 2 | 1 | 3 |
| **9** | 3 | 1 | 2 |
| **10** | 1 | 3 | 2 |

16–20

You are a conservative person who likes to be smart and well-dressed. You prefer darker colours, especially blues and greys. You only consider what you think is traditional and correct. However, your family and friends can buy a lot of clothes for you because they always know what to get you.

21–38

You are an enthusiastic reader of fashion magazines and would love to be able to wear the latest ideas. However, you usually buy what you see in the High Street shops. You have a lot of friends who wear the same clothes as you. Your favourite colours are white and green. You like casual clothes except for work when you think you should be smartly dressed.

39–48

You don't care about what people think and you wear what you like when you like. Your favourite colours are red and black but you don't look at the fashion magazines often because you like to be an individual. People often comment on your appearance. However, they are not always complimentary!

UNIT 2

# Folklore

## Listening/Reading: Little Red Riding Hood

**Cover the text and listen to it on the tape. Then answer the following questions:**

Who is the story about?

Do you recognise it?

Now listen a second time and tick whether the following statements are true or false:

| | Statement | TRUE | FALSE |
|---|---|---|---|
| 1 | The little girl lived in a forest. | | |
| 2 | She was taking food to her grandmother. | | |
| 3 | The girl's mother was ill. | | |
| 4 | The girl was lonely. | | |
| 5 | The girl was in a hurry. | | |

Once a long time ago there was a little girl who lived with her parents in a small village on the edge of a forest. Her father worked as a carpenter and her mother baked bread. She was a very pretty girl with long fair hair and bright blue eyes and she was often seen wearing a red cloak with a hood at the back made for her by her grandmother.

Her grandmother was a kind old woman with a lined face and grey hair which was always tied up in a bun, and although she lived alone in a small cottage in the middle of the forest she was liked by everyone in the village because she often helped people with their problems.

One day the girl's mother asked her to take some food to her grandmother who was ill. 'Go straight there, don't leave the path, and whatever you do, don't talk to any strangers,' she said.

The little girl set off carrying the basket. It was quite a warm autumn day and the sun was shining. The birds were singing and brown and gold leaves were being blown about in the wind. She passed through the village where people were working in their vegetable gardens or standing outside their front doors gossiping with their neighbours.

As soon as she entered the forest, though, she was quite alone. The little girl walked quickly along the path as she wanted to reach her grandmother's house as soon as possible. Suddenly she came across a wolf . . .

## Reading: Explanations

Read this passage and then answer the following question:

How many different explanations of folk tales are there in the text?

You can probably finish this story yourselves as this tale is told in different forms to children all over the world. Although it seems to be a simple, entertaining story for children, many people believe there is a hidden message. When it was first told years ago it was probably not just to children but to an adult audience too. Does Red Riding Hood in fact tell the story of a little girl growing up into a woman or does it show Day being eaten by Night? There are some people who think that folk stories such as this one are a way of coping with common worries and problems: others think they were the way early Man explained the working of Nature and the world. However, there are other interpretations, too. Is there a political message in these stories? Some people see a picture of the existing order of things, while others see a more radical picture of what a fairer society might be like. Perhaps these stories are an early form of science fiction. Or maybe there is a simpler explanation and after all they are just for amusement and pleasure.

Now read it again and choose ONE answer for each of the following questions:

**1** Red Riding Hood was
  **a** a secret story.
  **b** not suitable for children.
  **c** a true story.
  **d** told to different audiences.

**2** Fairy tales are
  **a** a record of what early man thought.
  **b** possibly about the future.
  **c** scientific explanations.
  **d** worrying and stressful.

## **Reading:** Guessing unknown words

### Advice on Reading Comprehension (Paper 1 Section B)

Guessing the meaning of unknown words:
If there is a word or several words that you do not understand in the text simply keep reading to get the general idea of the story, and guess the meaning from the clues in the text. You can use:

a) grammatical clues: is it a noun/verb/ adjective? etc.

b) contextual clues: the other information around it that you do understand. Is it to eat/ heavy/? etc.

### Exercise

Try guessing the meaning of these words from the text:

edge: is this an adjective or a noun?
does it tell you where something is or what it looks like?

baked: is this a noun or a verb?
is it something you do at home?
is it preparing food?

Now do the same with these words:

hood
cottage
path
strangers
leaves
set off
come across

## **Use of English:** Sentence transformation

Look at these two sentences:

*She was liked by everyone in the village.*
*Everyone in the village liked her.*

Do they have the same meaning?

Now find two sentences in the text with the same meaning as the ones below:

**1** People often saw her wearing a red cloak.

She ............................................................

**2** They tell this tale in different forms to children all over the world.

This tale ............................................................

### Advice on Use of English: Sentence transformation (Paper 3 Section A)

1. Read the first sentence carefully.
2. Your sentence must mean exactly the same as the first one.
3. Check you have included all the necessary information, and have used the correct tense and pronouns.

Finish the following sentences to mean the same as the ones printed above them.

**a** The Grimm brothers published hundreds of fairy stories.

Hundreds ......................................................

**b** They didn't invent some of them.

Some ...........................................................

**c** People handed down stories to their children.

Stories .........................................................

**d** They told the stories to explain how the world was.

The stories ...................................................

**e** Experts gave different explanations to these folk tales.

Different .......................................................

## **Writing:** Narrative

Compare these two passages:

When the actress and her companion walked into the restaurant everyone looked up. // They walked straight up to the centre table and sat down.

When the actress and her companion walked into the restaurant everyone looked up. She was wearing a very short, tight black dress with a wide belt. He was holding a tiny white dog in his arms. The dog was barking loudly and trying to get down. They walked straight up to the centre table and sat down.

Expand the following sentences to give more description and background.

1. I got home at seven o'clock last night and saw the whole family in the lounge. // I went upstairs to my bedroom.
2. I arrived at school late on my first day. // I apologised to the teacher and sat in the only empty chair.
3. We opened the door of the cafe and walked in. // We pushed through the crowd to the only free table.
4. He came out of the office into the busy main road. // He stopped a taxi and got in.

# **Use of English:** Gap filling

## Advice on Use of English: Gap filling (Paper 3 Section A)

In this part of the exam you are asked to fill in (20) missing words in a passage. There is only one word for each space (contractions count as two words). Some of the words you will know immediately but others you will have to guess. There are two things you can do to help you guess:

**1** First, read the whole passage without stopping and try to understand what it is about. If you have the general idea of the story guessing the missing words is much easier.

Example

In the colder ..........(1) of the world there are softwood forests. They contain thousands of ..........(2).

What is this text about? The answer is forests. You might have guessed the missing words already.

**2** Try to guess what type of word is missing, eg noun/verb/etc.

Example:

When I ..........(3) little my mother ..........(4) I planted ..........(5) baby tree ..........(6) the garden. It was ..........(7) to look at.

You can now have a better idea of which word is missing.

Now look at this passage and fill in the missing words. Remember to read it quickly first to find out what it is about. If you cannot think of the answer quickly decide what part of speech it is and then try to find what word is missing:

The detective got out of the taxi and crossed the road. He was ..........(1) a dark overcoat and a brown hat which he pulled down tight over his eyes. He walked into the cafe and sat down ..........(2) a table near the door. He took off his hat and lit a cigarette. The waitress ..........(3) sitting behind the counter. She was reading ..........(4) newspaper. She stood up and yawned, then she came over to ..........(5) detective's table. ..........(6) was wearing a black and white dress with a white apron that was creased and stained.

The detective looked up at her ..........(7) smiled. He ordered a ..........(8) of coffee.

A few moments later the waitress brought his order over to the table. She put the coffee in ..........(9) of the detective and left the bill under the saucer. He ..........(10) his coffee quickly and stood up, put some money on the table and walked out. It was raining and the street lamps were reflected in the puddles on the pavement.

## **Writing:** Description of a person

Look at this example question from Paper 2.

Composition: write a short description of a member of your family.

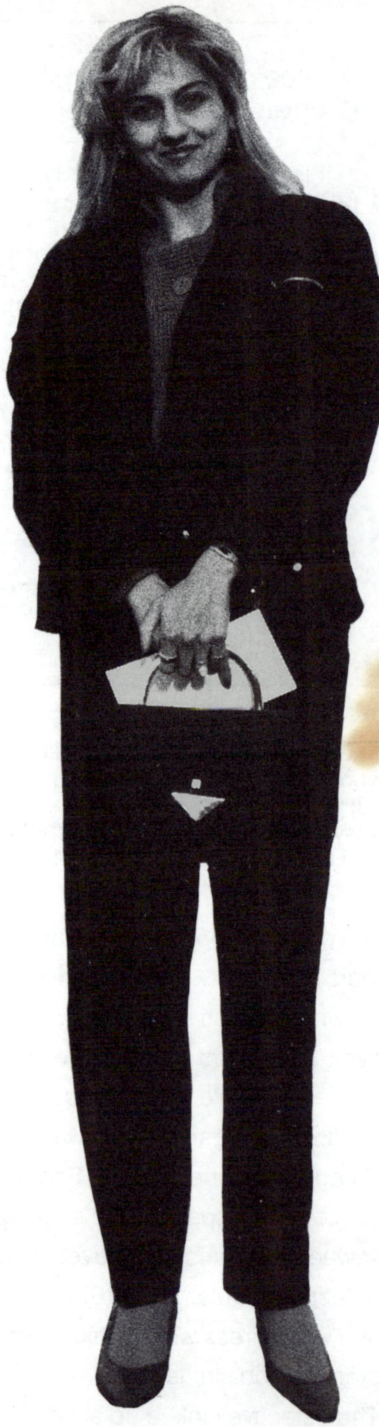

### Advice on Composition: Descriptions of a person (Paper 2)

The first paragraph is an introduction to the person, giving an idea of their appearance and what they do, who they are etc. without going into too much detail:

When my cousin Ana walks into a room everyone is immediately struck by her beautiful long hair and her stylish clothes. She is a slim woman in her twenties and as a model she has learnt to dress well and make an impression.

The second paragraph can then give more details:

Ana has in fact inherited her striking looks from her Indian mother who also has the same prominent cheekbones and deep brown eyes. However, Ana also resembles her father, especially in her height, as she is over 6 feet tall. She often emphasises her tanned skin with silver and turquoise jewellery and her long slender hands are usually decorated with several rings.

In the third paragraph you can develop characteristics other than the physical:

Ana has a lovely laugh and she often smiles. Yet sometimes you can see a faraway look in her eyes. Her most noticeable mannerism, however, which her friends often tease her about, is to flick away her hair from her face. Even when people ask about when she is going to get it cut she just laughs and promises never to take any notice of them.

Now write your own description of someone you know well.

## **Reading:** Multiple choice

### Advice on Reading: Multiple Choice (Paper 1 Section A)

Read each sentence carefully to make sure that you understand the meaning.

Try to think what the missing word is without looking at the four possible answers.

Do not spend too much time on each sentence: your first idea is usually correct. The longer you think about the possible answers, the more confused you can become!

**1** I grew .......... in Scotland and didn't move to the south until I was 8.
A out of B up C along D over

**2** My parents died when I was young and I was brought .......... by my grandmother.
A back B round C in D up

**3** She was a wise and wonderful woman, and I always looked .......... her.
A up to B down on C for D at

**4** Unfortunately, I didn't take .......... her. I was more like my father, who was not a very clever man.
A after B back C off D to

**5** She looked .......... me very well and I was a happy child.
A on B after C over D through

**6** She passed .......... when I was 17 and I suddenly felt very lonely.
A off B out C back D away

**7** After she died I came .......... a small fortune and with the money I started a business in London.
A across B out C into D down

**8** It wasn't long before I fell .......... a beautiful woman and we were married this spring.
A through B out C back on D for

## **Listening:** Fairy stories

### Advice on Listening: True/False questions (Paper 4)

In the time before you hear the passage concentrate on predicting the theme from the information you hear and the statement you are given (see Unit 1). You should also use whatever clues you can from the statements themselves. For example are the statements positive or negative, specific or general?

Listen to this radio programme about fairy stories and tick whether the statements alongside are True or False.

| | | TRUE | FALSE |
|---|---|---|---|
| 1 | Dr Johnson is interested in children. | | ✓ |
| 2 | The majority of people are told stories by a member of the family. | ✓ | |
| 3 | The most popular stories are not from storybooks. | ✓ | |
| 4 | Children prefer invented stories. | ✓ | |
| 5 | Fairy tales are more frightening than other stories. | | ✓ |
| 6 | The interviewer is not sure of the effect of frightening stories on children. | ✓ | |
| 7 | Children do not like sleeping on their own. | | ✓ |

## **Use of English:** Sentence transformation

*The monster was frightening*

*I was frightened*

### Transformations

In these exercises you must complete the second sentence so that it means exactly the same as the first.

### Exercise 1

**-ed/-ing**

Look at the two examples which have been done for you:

The story was very entertaining.
We were very entertained by the story.

I was surprised by the final scene.
The final scene was surprising

**1** The lesson was boring.

I ...............................................................

**2** I was terrified by the film.

The film ......................................................

**3** We were amused by his story.

His story .....................................................

**4** The ending was very frightening.

We were ......................................................

**5** His idea was interesting so I stayed to listen.

I was ..........................................................

### Exercise 2

**so / such . . . that**

Examples
It was such a frightening film that we walked out.
The film was so frightening that we walked out.

**1** It was such a cold day that we couldn't go out.

The weather ..................................................

**2** The book was so long that it took me ages to read.

It ...............................................................

**3** They were such friendly people that they invited us for lunch.

The people ...................................................

**4** The woman was so strong that I couldn't stop her.

She was .......................................................

**5** It was such a long film that I fell asleep.

The film was ..................................................

UNIT 3

# This changing World

## **Reading:** A bad weather forecast

**Read this leaflet and then answer the questions that follow:**

### * STOP CUTTING DOWN THE TREES!

Every minute of the day 100 acres of the world's tropical rainforests disappear. That's between 150–200,000 square kilometres a year. When these forests go you will lose between 50–90% of the world's plants, animals and insects. There is a simple answer: stop the cutting down of the trees so as not to lose them *completely* in 50 years' time. More than 40% of these forests have already gone. In 1950, 30% of the planet was covered by tropical rainforests. 25 years later only 12% was! It is even worse now and in 25 years' time it will probably be too late!

### * EVERYONE WILL SUFFER!

It is not only the natural world that will suffer. Do you know that one quarter of all medicines that you buy in the chemists' come from plants from the rainforests? Most of all, this environmental disaster of global proportions will fundamentally affect the way that you and everyone else live!

### * A WORLD UNDER WATER?

Scientists predict that what they call the 'greenhouse effect' will alter the weather patterns of the whole world. They expect the world will become warmer and warmer as the amount of carbon dioxide in the atmosphere increases. And what is one of the main causes of this? The destruction of the world's rainforests! Another is our insistence on burning up all our fossil fuels like coal, gas and oil. This increase in $CO_2$ will raise the temperature of the world's oceans. The polar ice caps will melt and the level of the seas will rise and rise! Only a small rise will threaten cities such as London, Venice and Bangkok. A rise of 5 metres of the Atlantic Ocean will flood the entire coastal regions of the eastern United States of America!!

### * SUPERPOWER STARVATION?

As well as the oceans the atmosphere will be affected too. Changes in rainfall patterns will mean the warm and dry regions of the world will become hotter and drier. Like Ethiopia now America and Russia will no longer be able to feed their own populations. On the other hand, areas

like the Middle East and the Indian sub-continent will become wetter and more fertile. Will the superpowers have to beg the Third World for food?

### * WORRIED? YOU SHOULD BE! WHAT ARE YOU GOING TO DO ABOUT IT?

Well, so as to preserve these crucially important resources you are going to have to decrease the amount of fossil fuels you use to run your car, heat your home and power your factory.

### * NO MORE HAMBURGERS?

So that you can eat your Macdonald's or Burger King double cheeseburger, acres of tropical rainforest have to be cleared to provide room for the cattle. What are you going to do about it?

### * IT'S YOUR CHOICE!

Are you going to think about the effect of your actions on the environment in order to leave our children a planet to live on? Or are you going to carry on letting the world die while you are making up your mind!!

### *** JOIN GREENSENSE NOW AND HELP SAVE THE PLANET!!!!! ***

Write to:– 500 York Buildings
Harrington
LONDON
NW5 5GN

Choose ONE answer for each of the following questions:

**1** Is the passage about
- **a** dying trees?
- **b** new medicine?
- **(c)** changing weather patterns?
- **d** changing eating habits?

**2** Between 1950 and 1975
- **a** 30% of the world's rainforest was lost.
- **b** 40% of the world's rainforest was lost.
- **(c)** The world lost 18% of its rainforests.
- **d** The world lost 12% of its rainforests.

**3** The 'greenhouse effect' will
- **a** endanger only coastal regions.
- **(b)** affect agricultural production in the USA.
- **c** cause famine in India.
- **d** make the whole world hotter and drier.

**4** Is the writer trying to
- **a** frighten the reader?
- **(b)** warn the reader?
- **c** amuse the reader?
- **d** confuse the reader?

## **Writing:** Link words of purpose

These are used when we want to explain why we are doing something.

**so as to in order to so that**

Look at these three examples:

The government is going to make lead-free petrol cheaper. More motorists will use it.

The government is going to make lead-free petrol cheaper **so that** more people will use it.

The UN will hold a conference on environmental problems. The UN wants to persuade every country to do more about pollution.

The UN will hold a conference on environmental problems **so as to** persuade every country to do more about pollution.

Greensense will demonstrate outside Parliament today.
Greensense wants to show its fears about the future.

Greensense will demonstrate outside Parliament **in order to** show its fears about the future.

Now do the same with the following pairs of sentences:
You may be able to use more than one phrase in each example but be sure to use each phrase at least once.

**1** I am going to London next year.
I want to improve my English.

**2** We are going to have a meeting with the Principal.
We want to complain about the canteen facilities.

**3** The government will introduce a new law.
Young people can work longer hours.

**4** The Council will buy up all the houses in the area.
The Council wants to build a new motorway.

**5** My father is going to buy a computer.
My brother can learn how to use a wordprocessor.

## Use of English: Expanded letter

### Advice on Use of English – Expanded Letters (Paper 3 Section A)

1 Read the COMPLETE letter through first – what follows a phrase or sentence may influence your choice of eg tense.

2 You will have to add auxiliary verbs, articles, prepositions, possessive pronouns etc. as well as writing the verbs out in full.

3 You do not have to change the word order.

Complete this letter sent to a newspaper by a reader worried about environmental problems. You will need to make changes and additions:

Dear Sir,

I/write/article/changing weather/last Tuesday's newspaper/and/I/like/agree/completely.

.......................................................................................................

**a** .......................................................................................................

We/must/stop/pollution/air/land/sea/or/planet Earth/die.

.......................................................................................................

**b** .......................................................................................................

We/have/stop/now/because/it/soon/too/late.

.......................................................................................................

**c** .......................................................................................................

What/governments/world/do/about/this?

.......................................................................................................

**d** .......................................................................................................

I/hope/other readers/agree/me/and/write/their/MPs/demand/action.

Yours faithfully

## Writing: Formal letters

Write the following letter:

You are interested in joining Greensense. Write to them asking about membership details.

## **Listening:** Holiday choices

Listen to this radio programme on five different holiday places and complete the details on the chart below:

| Destination | Average temperature | Maximum monthly rainfall | What to do and see |
|---|---|---|---|
| (1).......... | 30°+ | (2).......... | beautiful white (3)..........<br>green (4).......... forests<br>marvellous (5).......... |
| Thailand | (6).......... | over 50 cms | Buddhist (7)..........<br>beautiful (8).......... beaches |
| Peru | (9).......... | (10).......... on the coastal plain | Lake Titicaca<br>the (11).......... city of Machu Picchu |
| Soviet Union | 3° in Moscow and Leningrad | not stated | Moscow, Leningrad<br>(12).......... in the south |

## **Use of English:** Gap filling

Remember the advice given in Unit 2.

Read the text through quickly first and do not worry about words you don't know. You can always go back to them later. Even if you don't know a word try to guess what part of speech it is. NOTE: You can only put ONE word in each space.

Alaska ..........(1) not frozen all year round. Anchorage, ..........(2) largest city with ..........(3) population of less than 200,000, is hot ..........(4) dry during the summer with temperatures ..........(5) high as 30–35 °C. The south-eastern towns of Ketchikan and Sitka and the capital Juneau ..........(6) a relatively mild and rainy ..........(7) warmed ..........(8) the temperate air from the sea.

However, winters can be extremely cold. From late October ..........(9) early May the rivers are frozen and most ..........(10) Alaska is under snow. Without proper clothes you will ..........(11) survive. Some of the ..........(12) temperatures in ..........(13) world have been recorded ..........(14) this region.

If possible, visit ..........(15) the summer not just because of the warmer temperatures ..........(16) because of the midnight sun. The Arctic Circle, which is the line on which the sun never sets ..........(17) midsummer's day, passes north of Fairbanks. Even though this city is more than 180 kms ..........(18) of the Circle, the nights consist ..........(19) a brief twilight ..........(20) the early hours of the morning.

## **Communication Activity:** Reading passages

### Advice on Reading Passages (Paper 5 The Interview)

In the interview the examiner may ask you to read a short passage, but you will not have to read it aloud. Usually this is a starting point for a discussion. Try to read the passage quickly the first time to get an idea of the topic. The examiner may ask you where the passage comes from or why it was written or who is speaking. You may then be asked more general questions about the topic. Remember that you may ask the examiner questions too, especially if you do not understand a word or phrase or you do not know anything about the theme. The examiner does not know until you say. It is more important to show how much you can say rather than to be an expert on a particular subject.

Read the following passages and then be prepared to ask and answer questions about them. Your partner may help you.

**1** Hundreds of council workers were yesterday clearing up five miles of shoreline in West Wales polluted by a 100-tonne oil slick from a tanker. Wildlife experts were assessing the damage to swans and other seabirds. There were also fears that two salmon fish farms might have been affected.

**2** Bangladesh is a flat country, a delta dissected by hundreds of rivers and tributaries. The monsoon rains between June and September every year wash down tons of earth from the Himalayas. Many of the rivers are now too shallow to cope with the huge volume of water as they become filled with mud from the hills. Now the country is suffering from the worst floods in living memory.

**3** Flowers are an ornament that brighten the environment and make the world a happier place. They cannot always be planted directly in the ground and in such cases various containers can be used. For example, there are window boxes and hanging baskets. These are becoming more and more popular in towns and cities where there are few gardens.

# **Use of English:** Paragraph writing

## Advice on Use of English: Paragraph Writing (Paper 3 Section B)

In this part of the Use of English paper you are usually given some information in the form of notes, a diagram, a dialogue, a letter, a newspaper article etc. You are asked to interpret the information and write it in a different form. For example, you are asked to use the information to write a letter summarising the main points; list the advantages and disadvantages of a plan; or choose the best person for a job. To do this, you must use the information relevant to the question – not all the information given can be used.

There is often not just one correct answer: marks are given for a good answer with intelligent reasons and for the style of your answer (organisation, link words etc.).

**1** Read the information twice and underline or write notes on the relevant information.

**2** Write your answer using appropriate link words, including all the relevant points.

### Exercise

You live in Aberdeen in Scotland and would like the opportunity to go skiing occasionally. Look at the newspaper article and the notes on the three proposed sites for a new ski-resort, and complete the three paragraphs below, using approximately 60 words for each paragraph, giving reasons for your choice.

The Letsgo Company is proposing to build a modern, stylish ski-resort in the Scottish Highlands, an area covered in snow from November to March. They will construct chalets, high-rise hotels, a large leisure centre, shops and entertainment facilities, as well as ski lifts, cable cars and ski runs. It is hoped that the resort will attract over 8000 ski enthusiasts a year, and will provide at least 800 jobs during the two-year construction period and up to 200 winter jobs for local people when the resort is in operation.

There are three possible sites for the resort, each having climatic conditions and geographical location ideal for skiing. The company is currently deciding which of the three sites to develop. Their decision will take into account the interests of the environment and the local community.

Letsgo would like to hear comments and opinions of the sites from interested parties......

Notes:

Site 1

200 km north-west of Aberdeen
(4 hrs drive from Glasgow)
Densely forested area
Home of wild deer and rare birds
Very few inhabitants
Narrow roads, in bad condition
No railway
Strong winds from North Sea in autumn and winter

Site 2

80 km north of Aberdeen
(1½ hrs from Aberdeen Central Station and airport)
Very near Aberdeen reservoir – attractive lake
Popular area for picnics/walks in summer
Area of outstanding natural beauty
No trees
Good road and rail link to Aberdeen

Site 3

150 km west of Aberdeen
(2½ hrs from Aberdeen)
In Lochweel – farming village – cows and sheep use the slopes in the summer
High unemployment among young people – many move to Aberdeen to find work
No cinema, no disco
Quite good roads
No railway

**A** I think the Letsgo Company will choose site .............. because .......................................
.......................................................................
......... what's more, .......................................
.................. Although ..................................
.......................................................................

**B** I don't believe they'll choose site ................
because ......................................................
.......................................................................
.......................................................................
Another drawback is ....................................
.................. Although ..................................
.......................................................................

**C** I hope they won't choose site ......................
because ......................................................
................................................ Also, ..........
.......................................................................
besides, .....................................................
.......................................................................

## **Communication Activity:** Invitations

Work in pairs: Students A look at the information below. Students B look at the information on p. 33.

Following the information, practise the telephone conversations with your partner, using the appropriate language.

**1** You are going to the cinema tonight. You phone up your friend. Start the conversation.

**2** You are visiting your parents this weekend because it's your father's birthday.

**3** You are going to see the latest Rambo film at the cinema tonight because it is the last night.

**4** Your brother is having a party to celebrate his exam results. You want to invite one of the people you work with. Phone him/her.

## **Listening:** Invitations

Listen to these telephone conversations containing several invitations, acceptances and refusals and fill in the grid below with the missing information. Some of the answers have been done for you.

Exercise 1

| **Invitation** | **Relationship**<br>**a** inferior/superior (formal)<br>**b** colleagues – (semi-formal)<br>**c** friends – (informal)<br>**d** family – (informal) | **Response**<br>accept<br>refuse |
|---|---|---|
| 1.......... weekend at cottage | inferior/superior | 2.......... accept |
| 3.......... month's walking holiday | 4.......... friend | refuse |
| 5.......... motor yacht | 6.......... colleages | 7.......... refuse |
| 8.......... weekend at the seaside | 9.......... family | 10.......... accept |

Exercise 2
Now listen to the tape again and note down a suitable phrase in the right box.

| Useful language: | Formal | Semi-formal | Informal |
|---|---|---|---|
| Making invitations: | 1.......... | 2.......... | 3.......... |
| Accepting: | 4.......... | 5.......... | 6.......... |
| Refusing: | 7.......... | 8.......... | 9.......... |

## **Communication Activity:** Invitations

**Student B information**

**1**

You have decided to stay at home tonight because you are tired. The phone rings.

**2**

There is a new exhibition of Chinese art in London this weekend. You know one of your colleagues is very keen on Oriental art so you phone. Start the conversation.

**3**

You are having a dinner party tonight but suddenly one of your guests can't come because she's ill. A friend of yours has just moved into the area and doesn't know many people. Phone and invite him/her to the party.

**4**

You are feeling bored and would like to meet some new people. You don't know what to do tonight.

# Progress Test 1

## Paper 3: Use of English (2 hours)

### Section A

**1** Fill each of the numbered blanks in the following passage. Use only ONE word for each space.

He began ...... (1) walk up the drive ...... (2) I walked beside him, my legs suddenly heavy ...... (3) lead. The woman and the child followed behind ...... (4).

The cypress trees closed in around us, and the shuttered villa, like a tomb, waited ...... (5) the further end. As we approached I saw that it was large ...... (6) many windows, all of them blank and closed, and before the entrance the drive swept in ...... (7) circle for the carriages to turn. Statues ...... (8) their pedestals stood between the shrouded cypresses. The man ...... (9) the huge door with his ...... (10) and motioned me ...... (11). The woman and the child came too, and the ...... (12) of them began to open the shutters, letting the ...... (13) into the silent hall. The rooms all led into each other and were large and sparse with painted ceilings and stone ...... (14) and the air ...... (15) old and stale. In ...... (16) of the rooms the walls were plain and in others there were tapestries. In ...... (17) room which was darker and ...... (18) welcoming than the rest, there ...... (19) a long dining table with carved chairs and great iron candlesticks ...... (20) either end.

**2** Finish each of the following sentences in such a way that it means exactly the same as the sentence printed before it.

**Example**

I last saw him on my birthday.

I haven't *seen him since my birthday.*

**1** The factory will be closed down in two weeks.

They ..........

**2** The dessert was worse than the main course.

The main course ..........

**3** The horses were so friendly that they ate out of our hands.

They ..........

**4** We visited the cathedral and all the museums too.

As well as ..........

**5** No lake in the world is as low as the Dead Sea.

The Dead Sea ..........

**6** We rarely go on holiday these days.

We don't ..........

**7** How about coming to the cinema with us this evening?

Why ..........

8 She is his aunt.

He ..............................................................

9 He had a dark grey coat on.

He was ......................................................

10 Someone was watching him.

He was ......................................................

3 The words in capitals at the end of each of the following sentences can be used to form a word that fits suitably in the blank space. Fill each blank in this way.

**Example**

I have a company car, but I also have a car for my own .....personal..... use. PERSON

1 I know you think he's funny, but I don't think he's ........................... AMUSE

2 The fireworks made such a noise! My dog was ........................... TERRIFY

3 The centre of the country wasn't affected by the hurricane, but the ........................... areas were badly hit. COAST

4 The speech was so ........................... that I fell asleep. BORE

5 Much of the country's old woods and forests are being turned into ........................... land. AGRICULTURE

4 Complete the following sentences with one appropriate word connected with the subject of clothes.

**Example**

When he tried on the new pair of . . trousers . . he found they were too long and covered his shoes.

1 The field was wet and muddy, so they took off their shoes and put on their ..................... before walking across it.

2 He felt cold at first, but as he worked his hands became so hot he had to take off his

..............................................................................

3 The children were very sleepy and were sent upstairs to put on their .................................

4 It was raining and she didn't have an umbrella, but she put on her ........................ to keep her hair dry.

5 This isn't a suit – the ............................. isn't the same colour or pattern as the trousers.

5 Complete the following dialogue.

Paul: Hello, Frank, you look tired.

Frank: Yes, I know. I didn't get to bed until 2 this morning.

Paul: (1) What ...............................................?

Frank: I went to a party in London.

Paul: (2) Who ...............................................?

Frank: One of the people I work with. It wasn't his party, but he knew the hosts.

Paul: (3) Where ...........................................?

Frank: In North London, so it took me a long time to get home afterwards.

Paul: (4) Did ................................................?

Frank: Yes, I met a girl who I knew at school.

Paul: (5) Are ................................................?

Frank: Yes, I'm taking her to the cinema tomorrow.

## Section B

Study the plus points (++) and minus points (– –) of the four cars below. Then look at the people interested in buying a new car. Complete the paragraphs on page 37 explaining which car is suitable and which ones are unsuitable for the potential buyers.

**1**

October Road Test Report from CARMARKET magazine.
SCANVIA 377 GL estate.

++ A spacious car which can take up to 6 people in comfort. Lots of room to carry large loads in rear. Impressive safety features.

– – Expensive and heavy, it's a car the garage loves. Not recommended for parking, it's a beast to drive. Uncomfortable over 80 kph.

**2**

FAIRLEY ELITE 4×4
++ The ultimate business machine. Fast and luxurious with all latest refinements – ABS braking and CD player as standard. A car to make a good impression.
– – High on petrol. Very little room in back or boot – enough for overnight luggage only. Popular with insurance companies too!

**3**

KARMANN CONSTANT
++ The sensible car. Low on visits to petrol station or garage mechanic. Lifetime guarantee on spare parts from authorised dealers.
– – Not a car for the sensitive: it's reliable but noisy and uncomfortable. Two people fine but any more is a crowd. Very old-fashioned styling.

**4**

DAGMAR ALICIA LX
++ It's cheap and simple because not a lot can go wrong and it's not a favourite with car thieves or bank robbers so it's not going to be stolen. Quite a roomy car for its size – it can take 5 people maximum.
– – Difficult to drive with badly-designed controls. Easy to repair but it needs to be – it's very unreliable!

**A** Frank and Jane Givens, married with 3 children between 5–16. Both drive. Frank is doctor so needs reliable car that starts every day. Live in block of flats where parking is a problem. Often holiday abroad with children.

**B** Carl James, 24, salesman with international watch manufacturers. Needs car for work – has to travel long distances. Also enjoys weekends away with girlfriend. Enjoys repairing cars in his spare time.

Now complete the following paragraphs in no more than 50–60 words.

I think Frank and Jane Givens will buy a ......

..........................................................................

..........................................................................

..........................................................................

..........................................................................

..........................................................................

I think they definitely won't choose ..............

..........................................................................

..........................................................................

..........................................................................

..........................................................................

..........................................................................

I think Carl James will choose a ..................

..........................................................................

..........................................................................

..........................................................................

..........................................................................

..........................................................................

I don't think he will choose ..........................

..........................................................................

..........................................................................

..........................................................................

..........................................................................

..........................................................................

UNIT 4

# *Mysteries*

## Communication Activity: Describing photographs

Which pictures are these people talking about?

Talk about the pictures in the same way.

## **Listening:** The unbelievable

Listen to these people talking and tick the three pictures discussed.
Do you know anything about the stories behind the other pictures? Discuss in pairs or groups.

## **Use of English:** Sentence transformation

Rewrite these sentences to mean the same thing as the sentence before.

**1** It is said that he uses hypnosis.
People ..........................................................

**2** They claim that he is over 100 years old.
It ..........................................................

**3** They think that he can see into the future.
It ..........................................................

## **Reading:** Superstitions

These are two of the superstitions believed by many people in Britain:

If a black cat crosses your path, you will be lucky.

If you spill any salt you should throw some over your left shoulder or you will be unlucky.

What other superstitions do you know?

Now read about Geomancy – a Chinese belief.

**In the right place at the right time – the Chinese art of Geomancy**

*The picturesque landscapes of China were shaped by Feng-Shui experts. This palace illustrates some of the important geomantic elements: mountains at the back, water in the front and a pagoda on a hill to deflect harmful influences.*

***Skilled geomants*** *use an instrument called a* Feng-Shui *compass to help them determine the correct situation for building houses, tombs and other places. Concentrically arranged on the face of the compass is information relating to astrology, geographical direction, landscape features and symbols from the ancient* Book of Changes.

The idea that, if your house is built on the right position, this may affect your success in life seems strange to many people. However, to believers in Feng-Shui, or the art of geomancy, not only the position but also the choice of decorations and even the colour of your home can mean the difference between good fortune and disaster. This art has been practised for centuries in China and is still used all over South East Asia. Even the huge Hong Kong banks call in a geomant if they are planning to build new offices. They have such faith in his knowledge that if he advises them to move, they will alter their plans for even their biggest buildings.

Like many Oriental beliefs the geomant's skill depends on the idea of harmony in nature. If there is no imbalance between the opposing forces of Yin and Yang, the building will bring luck to its inhabitants. This means that the house must be built on the right spot as well as facing the right direction, and also be painted an auspicious colour. For instance, if there are mountains to the north, this will protect them from evil influences. If the house is painted red, this will bring happiness to the occupants, while green symbolises youth and will bring long life. Other factors, such as the owner's time and date of birth, are taken into account, too. The geomant believes that unless all these are considered when choosing a site for any construction, the fortune of the people using it will be at risk.

Indeed, to ignore the geomant's advice can have fatal results. The death of internationally famous Kung-Fu star, Bruce Lee, has been used as an example. It is said that when Lee found out that the house he was living in was an unlucky one, he followed a geomant's advice and installed an eight-sided mirror outside his front door to bring him good luck. Unfortunately, a storm damaged the mirror and the house was left unprotected from harmful influences. Soon afterwards Lee died in mysterious circumstances.

Not only is Feng-Shui still used in South-East Asia, but it has also spread right across the world. Even in modern New York a successful commercial artist called Milton Glaser has found it useful. He was so desperate after his office was broken into six times that he consulted a geomant. He was told to install a fish tank with six black fish and fix a red clock to the ceiling. Since then he has not been burgled once. It may seem an incredible story, but no other suitable explanation has been offered.

Now answer these questions:
Remember the advice from Unit 1.

1 What is Feng-Shui?
 **a** A style of Oriental decoration.
 **b** A type of painting.
 **c** An ancient Chinese belief.
 **d** An architectural design.

2 Where is Feng-Shui practised?
 **a** Only in China.
 **b** Only in Hong Kong.
 **c** Not just in New York.
 **d** Not just in South-East Asia.

3 Geomants believe that
 **a** horoscopes are important.
 **b** houses must only be painted red.
 **c** houses must face mountains.
 **d** green is an unlucky colour.

4 What did Bruce Lee do?
 **a** He consulted a geomant.
 **b** He moved out of his house.
 **c** He broke a mirror.
 **d** He died in a storm.

5 The story of Milton Glaser shows that
 **a** colours are not important in geomancy.
 **b** geomancy is used by artists.
 **c** geomancy is used in the West.
 **d** the fight against crime is being won.

## **Use of English:** Sentence transformation

1 He'll lose his way if you don't help him.
Unless ..........................................................

2 In the event of rain, the match will be cancelled.
If ..........................................................

3 He'll sign the contract on condition that he receives a substantial advance.
Provided ..........................................................

## **Vocabulary:** Prefixes and suffixes

### Un-/In-/Il-/Im-/-ful/-less

### I Prefixes

Prefixes **un-**/**in-**/**il-**/**im-** are added to the front of a word to make an opposite meaning, eg, patient → impatient.

Look at these words from the last Reading passage:

incredible l.55 unlucky l.39
imbalance l.18 unfortunately l.41

Which is the correct prefix for the words in capitals?

1 Why didn't you help him? It was very .......... of you.
KIND

2 You can't expect me to remember everything. It's just ..........
POSSIBLE

3 The government's decision to raise taxes was very ..........
POPULAR

4 Just sit still, I'll be ready in a moment. Don't be so ..........
PATIENT

5 He may come to the evening class, but he's still ..........
CERTAIN

6 I've got the same answers as he has, but a lower mark. It's ..........
FAIR

7 You'll never notice that mark on your coat. It's practically ..........
VISIBLE

**8** I had to get a new passport when I got married. My old one was .......... VALID

**9** I'd hate to live in a city with all that pollution. It's too .......... HEALTHY

**10** There are fewer and fewer jobs for .......... workers nowadays. SKILLED

**11** He didn't go to school. He can't read or write – he's .......... LITERATE

**12** He might pass his exam, but he doesn't work hard so it's .......... LIKELY

## II Suffixes

Look at the word *harmful* (1) in the Reading passage.

How can you make its opposite?

Some nouns can be made into adjectives by adding the suffixes -**ful** (meaning **with** or **giving**) and -**less** (meaning **without** or **not giving**) to the end of the word.

Here are some of those nouns.

How many of them *cannot* add *both* **less** and **ful**?

| | | |
|---|---|---|
| home | fault | harm |
| hope | help | pain |
| success | use | rest |
| thought | worth | regard |
| faith | power | sense |
| respect | skill | fruit |
| fear | care | joy |

# **Writing:** Link words

## Link words of Example and Link words of Connection

Look at how these link words are used in the Reading text on Geomancy.

for instance, (l.23)
such as (l.28)
not only . . . but also (l.46)
as well as (l.22)
also (l.23)
too (l.30)

Using these link words, complete the paragraph below.
Your choice will depend not only on the meaning but also on the structures.

The magician arrived early, long before the audience showed up. He had with him an enormous trunk containing various strange objects, ..........(1) colourful silk scarves, bunches of plastic flowers, a rabbit and a small electric piano. ..........(2) performing incredible magic tricks, he ..........(3) played a few songs to entertain the crowd. He wasn't just an ordinary magician. Of course he knew a number of well-known tricks, ..........(4) he could turn a scarf into a flower and back into a scarf again, but many other magicians can do that, ..........(5) This one was different. ..........(6) did he turn objects into plants, ..........(7) he could .......... turn himself into an object. Once, ..........(8), at the end of his show he suddenly disappeared and then, after a little while, when the audience was getting up to leave, he turned up at the back of the room as a chair and started shouting at the people, complaining that they were too impatient. He certainly was a very talented man!

Now choose one of these topics and write a short paragraph of about 60 words using some of the link words above:

Activities for visitors where you live
A zoo you once visited
National festivals
A successful year in your life
Bicycles

## **Communication Activity:** Describing photographs

Match the sentences 1–4 with the sentences a–d.

**1** He could be a Mexican.
**2** He must be a Mexican.
**3** He can't be a Mexican.
**4** He might be a Mexican.

**a** He's got a Mexican passport.
**b** He speaks Spanish.
**c** He lives in Mexico City.
**d** He only speaks French.

Information:

| | |
|---|---|
| Mexico | large country in Central America |
| Capital | Mexico City |
| Official language | Spanish |

Look at the pictures below and in pairs speculate on what they could be, using these phrases:

'It could be ..........' 'It must be ..........' 'It can't be ..........' 'It might be ..........'

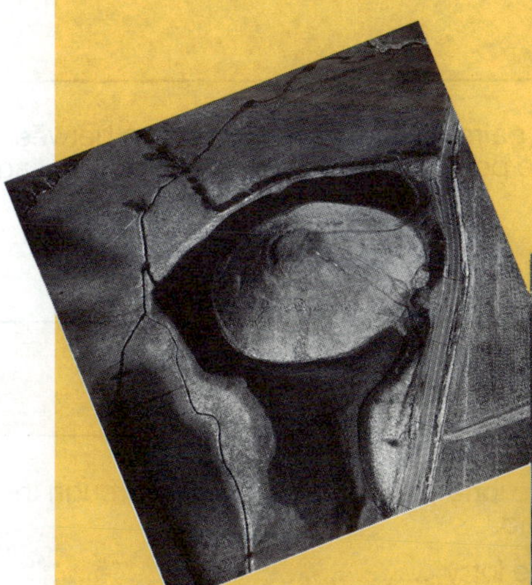

## **Communication Activity:** Reading passages

Look at the following extracts.
Where do you think you might see these?

**A** '. . . The present road system is quite sufficient to handle the volume of traffic in the area. I can see no reason why the authorities are planning to construct yet another motorway. It will ruin the countryside, encourage more people to use their cars instead of public transport and bring no benefits to the inhabitants of our town. On the contrary, should this plan be passed by the council, many local shopkeepers will lose a significant amount of trade. More importantly still, I understand from the plans that the by-pass will run directly over a site of great archaeological interest. . . .'

**B** '. . . I am writing to complain about a recent stay in your hotel. My wife and I booked a suite for the weekend, but on our arrival we were told that the hotel was full due to a conference of the UFO Society. We were eventually given a small room on the ground floor, but I am not satisfied with the way your employees treated us. . . .'

**C** '. . . I would like to complain about an incident during a holiday organised by your agency. I hired a local guide recommended by your brochure to show me around the sights and museums. However, the gentleman was unable to answer any of my questions concerning the history of the buildings or to give me any more information about the objects in the museums than was contained in the guidebook. I will not take this matter any further provided that you agree to refund the fee I paid for the guide. . . .'

**D** '. . . At a meeting yesterday villagers expressed their concern at the large numbers of tourists visiting their town in the hope of seeing the so-called monster in the lake. The inhabitants are protesting against recent newspaper reports publicising several sightings of the creature by a local fisherman. Mr Gaitshead, the fisherman concerned, was present at the meeting and agreed to show evidence of his claims. . . .'

## **Listening:** Complaints

**1** You will hear three dialogues, A, B and C. Match the dialogues to three of the letters above.

**2** In pairs, act out the conversation between the people concerned in the other passage.

## **Use of English:** Sentence transformation

Complete the following sentences to mean the same as the ones printed above them.

**1** We couldn't hear the speaker because the room was too noisy.

The room ....................................................

**2** The lorry was too wide to pass through the road.

The lorry ....................................................

**3** The dining table couldn't fit into the kitchen.

There wasn't ....................................................

## **Writing:** Informal letters

### Advice on Composition: A letter to a friend (Paper 2)

Remember that for most letters you are replying to someone (even if it does not actually say so in the title) so you can use this to help you write the opening paragraph. Here, for example your friend has written to you about his/her first day at school.

The main part of the letter is concerned with what YOU want to say. In this answer you are told to tell your friend about *your* first day. What are you going to write about? How did you feel? What were the other students/the teachers/the school/classes like? What did you do? etc. You also want a reply to your letter so in the closing paragraph you can ask your friend to write to you/come to see you etc or maybe suggest doing something together.

Finally don't forget to end the letter with a suitable AND appropriate phrase.

Put these phrases in the correct order.

**a** We are very happy in our house now.
**b** Looking forward to hearing from you all soon.
**c** Thanks very much for your letter.
**d** 21 Cope Street
Brighton
East Sussex
**e** It was great to hear from you again after such a long time.
**f** Well, enough about me, what is your news?
**g** Best Wishes
**h** It is wonderful news about your new job!
**i** Dear Jack
**j** The children are enjoying their new school and it is so much easier for me to get to work in the mornings!
**k** 21st May 1990
**l** We hope you can come and see us again this summer.

**1**
**2**

**3**
**4**
**5**
**6**

**7**
**8**

**9**
**10**
**11**

**12**

## **Composition:** The very first day

Your pen friend has written to you describing his/her first day at school. Reply to the letter and tell him/her about your first day.

UNIT 5

# Lifestyles

## Reading: Success

Discuss with your partner what kind of business you would like to run and why.

### BRANSON: Discovering Virgin Territory

In 1968 Richard Branson was an enthusiastic but rather shy 17-year-old in scruffy clothes, hard at work in a dark untidy basement. Newspaper articles of the time described the launch of a new glossy magazine, 'Student', the first national magazine for young people at school and at university and its teenage founder, Richard Branson.

My interview with him is twenty years later in his houseboat on London's Regent's Canal, and although his successes since 1968 have made him a multi-millionaire, the man himself hasn't changed much. Surrounded by men in dark suits, this high-powered businessman is wearing a loose knitted sweater and jeans and appears to be relaxed and friendly.

He seems an unlikely millionaire. He is casual and quiet, genuinely courteous and modest. He also appears to be very honest about his terror of public appearances. We are talking in his office in the houseboat. It is a homely, cluttered room, with pine furniture, reached by a short climb up a narrow staircase. In the room below two secretaries sit in the middle of piles of papers, typewriters and telephones. Branson calls down messages through the open door and the secretaries call back. It is an informal way of working and it seems to suit him.

After 'Student' magazine, Branson started a small mail-order record business in the early 1970s, with its headquarters over a shoe shop.

Today the Virgin group is worth hundreds of millions of pounds. It is one of Britain's leading record companies and Branson has expanded into the entertainment field, with nightclubs and satellite TV stations, and even owns an airline. Yet the company name was chosen because he knew nothing about the business when he started.

His sense of adventure extends from his professional life into his leisure interests. He has twice attempted to cross the Atlantic in record-breaking times – once, successfully, by speedboat in 1986, and once by hot-air balloon in 1987 when he failed, however, to repeat his earlier triumph and his balloon was rescued off the coast of Ireland.

He admits he is a workaholic but he keeps his weekends special and usually spends them quietly with his family at his country home. He always gets out of London by Friday night and never takes work home. He is a keen sportsman and plays tennis and golf, though surprisingly he rarely listens to music and wasn't sure where the record-player was.

He has, in fact, only had one well-publicised commercial failure since he started – the collapse of his short-lived London magazine 'Event'. His major talent is for original ideas and choosing the right people to work for him. Then he can leave the everyday running to them and concentrate on what he enjoys most – creating more new ideas. Virgin comes up with one every fortnight, he says, and his own mind is obviously overflowing with new schemes. Having come this far so successfully there seems little reason for Richard Branson to change either his lifestyle or his business methods.

## Multiple-choice questions

**1** 'Student' magazine

**a** was not written for people in employment.
**b** was an educational magazine.
**c** made Branson a millionaire.
**d** was discovered by Branson in 1968.

**2** Richard Branson

**a** still wears the same clothes.
**b** doesn't like working in tidy offices.
**c** dislikes appearing on radio and TV.
**d** has lived on a houseboat for 20 years.

**3** Virgin

**a** is a multi-million pound record company.
**b** started out as a shoe shop.
**c** was started because Branson knew nothing about selling records.
**d** has grown enormously in its first 15 years.

**4** Branson

**a** has made the two fastest crossings of the Atlantic.
**b** holds the record for the fastest Atlantic sea crossing.
**c** was rescued by balloon in 1987.
**d** has broken records in his business life as well as his free time.

**5** Branson

**a** does not discuss his work with his family.
**b** enjoys running his companies.
**c** is a good employer.
**d** has been successful with almost all his business schemes.

## **Vocabulary:** Word building

Compound words:

Look at these words from the passage: houseboat, businessman, sportsman, everyday, staircase.

How many compound words can you make beginning with the words in capitals? Can you put them into a sentence to show what they mean?

Examples:
to overwork = to work too hard
overtime = I did an hour's overtime last night because I need the money.

| | |
|---|---|
| OVER<br>HEAD<br>TOOTH<br>HAIR<br>HAND<br>HOUSE<br>LAND<br>RAIN | lord, brush,<br>work, line, paste,<br>ache, bow, take,<br>keeper, fall,<br>dresser, land,<br>quarters, writing,<br>time, shake,<br>wife, lady, hold,<br>out, look |

How many words can you make which end in the words in capitals?

| | |
|---|---|
| snow,<br>house,<br>sales,<br>watch,<br>ship,<br>thunder,<br>trades,<br>horse | MAN<br>KEEPER<br>STORM<br>WRECK |

## Word search

Find words or phrases in the text that mean the opposite of the following:

**1** sociable
**2** smart
**3** organised
**4** tense
**5** formal
**6** impolite
**7** bare and unwelcoming
**8** unenthusiastic

## **Writing:** A speech of introduction

Example question
You have been asked to introduce a guest speaker at a dinner/conference. Write your speech in between 120 and 180 words.

### Advice on Writing a Formal Speech (Paper 2)

You must remember two things when answering this type of question. Firstly your answer must be properly planned and laid out and secondly you must use the correct language for this type of writing.

Look at this sample answer using information about Richard Branson.

| | Useful language |
|---|---|
| First paragraph: Introduction, name and title of Guest Speaker<br><br>Mr Richard Branson | Ladies and gentlemen, good evening, I'm delighted to be here tonight to welcome our guest speaker, .......... |
| Main body of speech: **a** facts<br><br>successful businessman, lives on house boat, multi-millionaire, owns airline, | As you all know .............................................. |
| **b** achievements/ experiences<br><br>built up business group, expanded into entertainment field, become famous outside work for attempts on Atlantic records | First of all I'd like to tell you something about Richard. During his career he .................................... and in his personal life he has .............................................. |
| **c** examples with dates<br><br>started with 'Student' magazine in '68, broke record for sea crossing in 1986, tried to cross by balloon in 1987, | we all remember in 19xx he .............................................. and in 19xx .............................................. |
| Final paragraph: closing remarks and announcement:<br><br>reputation as shy man who prefers to be with family, agreed to be here because supports charity. | I would like to finish by saying .............................................. It gives me great pleasure to introduce .............................................. |

Follow-up

Now write a speech to introduce ONE of the following in approximately 100 words:

a famous explorer
a long-serving teacher
a famous athlete/sportsman/woman
a person of interest to you/the class

## **Communication Activity:** Vocabulary

What makes a successful **a** TV newsreader,
**b** journalist,
**c** salesman/woman?

Work in pairs and, using the list below, choose five qualities which are the most important, and five qualities which are the least important for each of the occupations above.

| | | | | |
|---|---|---|---|---|
| A newsreader needs to be: | determined<br>intelligent | punctual<br>optimistic | enthusiastic<br>realistic | A newsreader doesn't need to be: |
| A journalist needs to be: | courageous<br>experienced<br>friendly | charming<br>talented<br>hard-working | energetic<br>serious<br>sensitive | A journalist doesn't need to be: |
| A salesman/ woman needs to be: | imaginative<br>good-looking<br>ambitious | organised<br>clever<br>quick-thinking | sympathetic<br>sensible<br>calm | A salesman/ woman doesn't need to be: |

## **Vocabulary:** Word building

### dis-/mis- prefixes

These prefixes can be placed before verbs to indicate negation or incorrectness. Complete the sentences using a form of the word in capitals:

**1** I .................... with you about the Channel Tunnel. I don't think it will be dangerous at all. (AGREE)

**2** I .................... living in the city because it is so noisy and dirty. (LIKE)

**3** My gold bracelet has ....................! I can't see it anywhere. (APPEAR)

**4** I think you must have .................... I said £15, not £50! (HEAR)

**5** You have .................... the address. There is no Mr Brown living here. (TAKE)

**6** He .................... the number of guests and only bought enough wine for ten people. (CALCULATE)

**7** He .................... the instructions and pressed the wrong button. (UNDERSTAND)

**8** I was .................... by the poor condition of the house and thought he had no money. (LEAD)

## **Listening:** Talking about home

Ask other students in the class what type of house or flat they live in and how long they've been living there, what they particularly like about their home or area and where they lived before.

Now listen to these three people talking about their homes and answer the questions.

### Multiple-choice exercise

Remember only ONE answer is possible.

**1** The first couple
**a** were married 15 years ago.
**b** have had to move the coffee table many times.
**c** have had the picture for 10 years.
**d** have bought all their furniture.

**2** The second house
**a** has seven bedrooms.
**b** was originally part of a farm.
**c** has animals in the garden.
**d** has only one bedroom.

**3** The second couple
**a** have been decorating the spare room in their free time.
**b** have travelled all over the country in a caravan.
**c** have spent 10 years working on the house.
**d** have finished all the bedrooms.

**4** The painting in the second house
**a** was finished in 1813.
**b** faces the window.
**c** was painted by a member of the family.
**d** is the only cheap thing in the room.

**5** The speaker in the last passage
**a** is a professional decorator.
**b** has paid for everything himself.
**c** can't afford new furniture.
**d** has spent five years working on the flat.

## **Use of English:** Verb forms

**Exercise 1**

Look at this passage, where James Brown talks about his life with travel writer, Silvia Brown. Write out the verbs in brackets (in full).

We (**1** live) all over the world – Kenya, India, the States, but we (**2** come) back to this country in 1970, and we (**3** live) in Northolt ever since. My wife is a travel writer, she (**4** write) about all the wonderful places we (**5** be) in and the articles (**6** be published) in a variety of magazines. Now she's trying to write her fifth novel which she's finding difficult. She (**7** write) it for about six months now. She (**8** complete) the first and last chapters and now she's trying to write what happens in the middle, but that seems to be a problem.

**Exercise 2**

### Incomplete Dialogue

Now imagine you are interviewing Mr Brown.

Refer to the paragraph above and write the appropriate questions for his answers.

**1** You: How ..................................................?
Mr Brown: Since we came back in 1970.

**2** You: What other countries ..........................?
Mr Brown: All over the world – Kenya, India, the States.

**3** You: Where ..................................................?
Mr Brown: In a variety of magazines.

**4** You: How ..................................................?
Mr Brown: Four.

**5** You: How ..................................................?
Mr Brown: For about six months now.

**6** You: How ..................................................?
Mr Brown: The first and last chapters.

**Exercise 3**

### Sentence transformation

Complete the following sentences to mean the same as the ones printed above them.

**1** We bought that sofa on our first wedding anniversary.

We've ..................................................

**2** We moved here 50 years ago.

We've ..................................................

**3** We've been working on the house for 10 years.

We started ..................................................

**4** It's ages since we've had some free time.

We haven't ..................................................

**5** It's years since we last saw him.

We haven't ..................................................

**6** You haven't been here for 10 years.

It's ..................................................

## **Vocabulary:** Problems with the phone

Put these expressions into the correct places in the dialogues below:

| | |
|---|---|
| rang up | ring back |
| call back | speak to |
| cut off | get through |
| hold on | asking for |
| put me through to | |

**A:** Could you (1).......... Mr Jones in the Sales Department, please?

**B:** I'm sorry, sir, the line's engaged. Do you want to hold?

**A:** No, I'll (2).......... later.

**A:** Could I (3).......... Mr Jones in Sales, please.

**B:** (4).........., sir, I'll try to connect you.

**C:** Sales Department.

**B:** Someone is (5).......... Mr Jones.

**C:** He's not in this afternoon. The office is closed.
Ask the caller to (6).......... tomorrow.

**A:** Mr Jones please.

**B:** Which department?

**A:** Sales. I (7).......... yesterday but couldn't (8)..........

**B:** One moment, sir.

**D:** Sales Department.

**A:** Ah. Is that Mr Jones?

**D:** Speaking.

**A:** I have a complaint to make about my bill.

**D:** (hangs up)

**A:** Hello, hello. This is ridiculous. I've been (9).......... I only wanted to tell them they've undercharged me.

## **Writing:** Formal letter

### Letter of Application

Look at these jobs advertised in various newspapers.

Choose the one you would most like to apply for and then complete the letter below giving details of relevant experience, previous employment and your interests.

You don't want to be turned down, so use your imagination to make your letter of application interesting to the employer.

Major international airline looking for good-looking, polite young people to train as stewards/stewardesses on transatlantic flights. Salary negotiable.

Premier recording studio has urgent vacancy for fully-qualified engineer to work on top name bands.
Competitive rates.

Barman/bar maid wanted for top London night spot. Experience needed but uniform provided. Good pay and late meal included.

Talented guitarist needed for hit band. Must be able to play pop, rock and roll and jazz styles and be available for world tour.
Substantial share in profits.

Dear Sir,

I am writing to apply for the post of (1).......... advertised recently in your newspaper. I believe I have the relevant experience to qualify for the job as I have been working as a..........(2).......... for ..........(3).......... I have also .......... (4).......... and .......... and I can also ..........(5).......... I am interested in ..........(6)..........

I am available for interview at any time convenient for you.

I look forward to hearing from you.

Yours faithfully

.......................................................

## **Communication Activity:** Going for an interview

You are now going to interview each other for the jobs. In pairs, decide who is going to be the employer and who the applicant.

Employers

You are going to interview candidates for one of the posts advertised above.

Decide

what type of person you are looking for

what skills and experience are necessary

what questions you can ask the applicants

the salary, hours of work, holiday etc.

Applicants

You have been asked to attend an interview for the job you applied for.

Decide

why you are suitable for the job

what questions you can ask the interviewer (eg salary, hours of work, holidays)

## **Writing:** Discursive composition

### For and against

Home is where the work is.

What are the advantages and disadvantages of working from home with a computer?

> **Discursive composition (Paper 2) Advantages and disadvantages**
>
> This type of composition demands a simple statement of advantages and disadvantages. Make sure you list your points for and against the topic before going on to writing the composition. You should include a general introduction and a general or personal conclusion.

**1** Look at this passage and list the advantages and disadvantages the writer thinks there are in working at home.

More and more people nowadays have computers in their homes and are using them both for games and, increasingly, for work.

One advantage of working from home is that people can choose where they live rather than try to be near the office. Another point in its favour is that the stresses of commuting to work by train or car disappear, and people can get to work simply by switching on their computer screens. Moreover, mothers and fathers can spend more time at home with their children.

On the other hand, there are several disadvantages. One drawback is the danger of isolation as the daily contact with colleagues in the office is lost. What's more, houses need to be more spacious, with an extra room to use as an office. Another point worth noting is the possible conflict between the demands of the family and the pressures of work.

Personally, I believe that on the whole the advantages outweigh the disadvantages, and I would enjoy working from home.

**2** Discuss with a partner the possible advantages and disadvantages of the following topics:

**a** Discuss the advantages and disadvantages of retiring early.
**b** No-one should do any one job for longer than five years.
**c** What are the advantages and disadvantages of being self-employed?

**3** Now write between 120 and 180 words on one of these topics.

UNIT
6

# Sport

## Listening: 'Sports News'

Find someone in the class who

**a** has taken up a new sport recently
**b** belongs to a team or a club
**c** plays an unusual sport
**d** prefers watching sport

Now listen to this radio interview about sport between the 'Sports News' presenter and Chris Michaels, a young sportsman. For questions 1–8 tick whether the statements are true or false.

| | | TRUE | FALSE |
|---|---|---|---|
| **1** | Chris is a professional athlete. | | |
| **2** | He has a competition shortly. | | |
| **3** | He doesn't have to train every day. | | |
| **4** | He has suffered minor injuries. | | |
| **5** | He sometimes finds it difficult to keep to his schedule. | | |
| **6** | Chris believes it is good to start training when you are young. | | |
| **7** | He believes that no-one can make children train too hard. | | |
| **8** | The interviewer agrees with all he says. | | |

## Use of English: Sentence transformation

Rewrite the following sentences to mean the same as the sentence above.

**1** It is essential to have a balanced diet.

You ..........................................................................

**2** It is not necessary to give up your job to be a champion.

You ..........................................................................

**3** It is important not to train too hard.

You ..........................................................................

**4** It is not vital to take extra vitamins.

You ..........................................................................

**5** It is necessary to keep training every day.

You ..........................................................................

## **Vocabulary:** Parts of the body

### Exercise 1

Look at the illustration and label as many parts of the body as you can.
Check your answers with a partner.

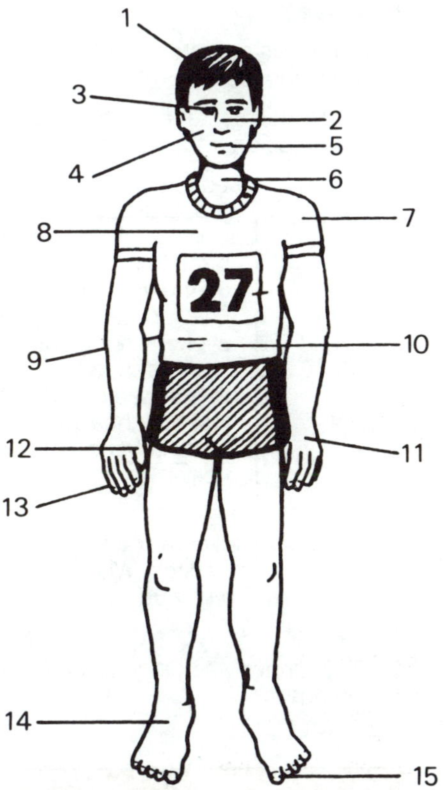


### Exercise 2

Now look at these sentences.

Each contains a verb made from a part of the body.

Using the diagram, the context and your own imagination, decide what the meaning of the sentence is.

Example

He couldn't see the match so he **elbowed** everyone **out of the way** until he reached the front of the crowd.

He made a path for himself through the crowd using his elbows.

1 The crowd **headed for** the exit after the final whistle.

..........................................................................

2 After the game the buses were very crowded so he tried to **thumb a lift** to London.

..........................................................................

3 The Cuban boxer came out of his corner so fiercely that the American had to **back away**.

..........................................................................

4 It is important in a relay race to **hand over** the baton quickly and smoothly.

..........................................................................

5 Although the referee didn't see, thousands in the crowd saw the attacker **mouth the words** at the defender lying on the ground.

..........................................................................

6 Having won his semi-final he now **faced** the champion in the final.

..........................................................................

### Exercise 3

Now look at these sentences. Here the verbs are not being used in such a literal or obvious way, but you should still be able to guess their meaning.

1 It's great fun staying in the Olympic village, especially when someone else is **footing the bill**.

2 He now **heads the list** of all-time fastest runners over 1500 metres.

3 It's not just the athletes who have to **shoulder the responsibility** for drug taking during these events.

4 She **eyed up** the rest of the field and thought she had a good chance of a medal.

5 He waited impatiently for the game to start and **thumbed through** the programme to see the kick-off time.

6 As the national anthem was played she **fingered** her gold medal nervously.

### Exercise 4

These words are often used in other expressions too.

Look at these sentences and fill in the gaps with one expression from the box.

Each can be used in only ONE sentence.

| |
|---|
| back to front<br>on the tip of my tongue<br>stick my neck out<br>from head to toe<br>to be nosey<br>lost their heads<br>hand in hand<br>tiptoe |

1 The horse fell at the last fence and the rider fell off into the ditch. When she got up she was covered in mud .................................... ....................................................

2 The runner was disqualified for wearing his number ..................................................

3 Advertising contracts and sponsorship deals usually go .......................................... with winning a gold medal.

4 I can't remember who the last man to break the world record for a marathon was. Oh, wait a minute, it's .......................................... ..................................................., I'll think of it in a moment.

5 When the judges gave the decision in favour of the other team, all the players ................ ................................................... and started hitting the officials and shouting at them.

6 During her floor exercises, the gymnast's routine was so graceful and calm that at one point she almost seemed to ..................... across the floor.

7 I know it's not a very easy race to pick a winner, but I'm going to .......................... ................................................... and choose the Russian.

## **Reading:** The Olympic Games

How often are the Olympic Games held?

When are the next Games?

Where are they being held?

Is there a limit to what the human body can do?

*altius, citius, fortius*

To go higher, to go faster and to be stronger

These are the words written around the Olympic flame, burning in the latest ultra-modern stadium, the latest venue of one of the most outstanding spectacles in the world. Each day thousands in their seats in the stadium and millions in their chairs at home watch excitedly as men and women from almost every nation in the world attempt to run faster, jump higher and longer, lift heavier and heavier weights and throw further and further. They are all competing for that ultimate prize: an Olympic gold medal. Some only just fail by hundredths of a second or fractions of a millimetre but are content with a silver or bronze. Most are extremely happy just to be there and in so doing agree with the other motto of the Games which says that it is not winning that is important but taking part.

However, as the Olympics reach the end of the 20th century and look forward to the 21st, it seems as if this second ideal is no longer a realistic one for our competitive world. Much as we are happy to see the medals won, especially if they are won by our compatriots, it is not enough. What the crowd badly wants to see is records being broken. We all want to witness that moment in history when something is achieved for the very first time.

Yet in this search for greater achievement we are seriously in danger of losing the very ideal of the Olympic Games and possibly of sport in general. We are no longer content to see men and women try their hardest having trained themselves to the peak of their performance; we demand new records. Although we criticise them for doing so, turning to drugs may be the only way some athletes see of satisfying the public's hunger.

Even though we pretend that the Olympic's are still the last preserve of the amateur ideal, we know that to be a world-class athlete now is a full-time activity. It is not only the intensive training given to potential champions by the super-powers, but many athletes are paid now. Since 1982 the International Olympic Committee has allowed money from appearances and advertising to be kept for the competitor until he or she retires and even used for training purposes and expenses.

Are we pushing the athletes too hard? Can we expect the athlete to live up to the ideal of the Games without the help of modern science and technology? Indeed, how much further can the human body go? Records continue to be broken but increasingly by smaller and smaller margins. Will we reach the stage of seeing someone run the fastest, jump the highest and throw the furthest that it is humanly possible to do? Is it too late to go back to the pure ideals of the ancient Games or is it just another part of our life that is increasingly dominated by technology?

Choose the answer which best completes the sentence:

**1** Competitors at the Olympics want to
**a** entertain the spectators in the stadium and at home
**b** perform better than anyone else in the field.
**c** come as close as possible to the fastest time.
**d** do more than just participate.

**2** According to the writer, the second motto of the Olympic Games
**a** will be dropped in the 21st century.
**b** does not satisfy the general public.
**c** has been overtaken by the first motto.
**d** is too idealistic.

**3** Non-competitors desire most strongly to see
**a** their countrymen and women win a first prize.
**b** a world record being broken.
**c** athletes perform to the best of their ability.
**d** an Olympic record being broken.

**4** Taking drugs may help athletes
**a** to eat more.
**b** to perform better.
**c** to be critical.
**d** to train less.

**5** The International Olympic Committee
**a** prevents amateurs from entering the Games.
**b** makes athletes pay to enter the Games.
**c** lets athletes be paid to enter the Games.
**d** lets athletes use the money earned from commercials.

**6** The writer believes that
**a** it will become more difficult to break records.
**b** the Olympic ideals will not be followed.
**c** we must force athletes to train harder.
**d** athletes can continue to break records without resorting to drugs or technology.

## Cohesion: Understanding references

It is difficult to understand a passage if you don't see the connections between the words in a sentence and between sentences. Some words refer backwards, some look forwards.

What do these words refer to in the text?

**1** they l.10

**2** there l.15

**3** this ideal l.20

**4** one l.21

**5** so l.35

## **Writing:** Link words of concession, cause and result

Look at these pairs of sentences:

**1** **a** **Although** it was raining heavily, they went on playing.
**b** **Because** it was raining heavily, they stopped playing.

**2** **a** **Even though** there was a gale blowing, the boats set sail.
**b** **As** there was a gale blowing, the race was cancelled.

**3** **a** **Owing to** severe frostbite on his hands he had to abandon the climb.
**b** **In spite of** severe frostbite on his hands he reached the summit.

**4** **a** **As a result of** his injury he had to give up his training.
**b** **Despite** his injury he continued his training.

**5** **a** The horse was exhausted, **but** it still won the race.
**b** The horse was exhausted, **so** it could only manage second place.

**6** **a** Cricket is essentially an Englishman's sport. **Therefore**, it is not played world-wide.
**b** Cricket is essentially an Englishman's sport. **However**, it is popular in many other countries.

**7** **a** The equipment for this sport is wildly expensive. **Consequently**, few people can afford to play it.
**b** The equipment for this sport is wildly expensive. **Nevertheless**, some clubs exist in even the poorest areas.

**8** **a** **Since** it is very popular here the American Football match attracted many spectators.
**b** **Because of** its popularity the American Football match attracted many spectators.

1 Which link words are used to introduce a logical reason?

2 Which link words are used to introduce an illogical reason?

3 Which link words are used to introduce the logical result?

4 Which link words are used to introduce the illogical result?

Complete this passage using the link words above.

Tottenham have had a disappointing start to the season, (1).......... they will need to play especially well to hold their supporters' attention in the coming matches. Yesterday's performance against Nottingham confirmed their ability to work hard, (2).......... they are still making some serious mistakes. It was mainly (3).......... their new goalkeeper's errors that they were beaten 2–0.

26-year-old Eric Thorstredt was replacing Bobby Mimms, who had to withdraw from the match (4).......... a dislocated shoulder. Eric has not been in the team long. (5).........., much more was expected from him than his performance against Nottingham. Things looked bad from the beginning. (6).......... his height, he was not able to stop several shots during the warm-up before the match started. (7).......... the rest of the team were playing well, he never seemed sure of himself and after 20 minutes let an easy shot slip through his hands. During the second half, Nottingham's Bob Peterson broke through Tottenham's defence, and (8).......... Eric had plenty of time to block it, he was unable to prevent the score being brought to 2–0.

## **Writing:** Discursive composition

### Giving an argument

This is part of a composition on the importance of money in sport.

Look at the expressions in *italics*:

*On the one hand* the Olympics are supposed to offer equal opportunities to all, *but on the other (hand)* it is very difficult too for countries with a limited budget to compete with the larger, wealthier nations.

However, although most of the gold medals are won by the superpowers, there are often surprise winners from smaller, less well-off countries. Nevertheless, it is easier to be a winner if you have the considerable resources and expertise of the USA or USSR behind you. Even though we might dream of the ordinary man or woman in the street beating the rest, it is no coincidence that the world records are held by athletes from a fairly limited number of countries.

> It is also important to give your opinion about the topic clearly. You can use these words or phrases:
>
> In my opinion ..........................................
> I feel that ..................................................
> Personally, I think ....................................
> People should/shouldn't ...........................

Write about one of the following topics trying to use these expressions. They will help your composition to have balance.

1 Winning is not important in sport.

2 It should not be countries competing in the Olympics, just athletes.

3 Sport has no place in schools.

## Listening: Giving instructions

You are going to hear someone talking about kite flying. Tick the boxes true or false.

| | | TRUE | FALSE |
|---|---|---|---|
| 1 | Kite flying has been used for wartime and peacetime activities. | | |
| 2 | It is a popular hobby among western adults. | | |
| 3 | Kites can't fly if they aren't light enough. | | |
| 4 | Bamboo is perfect for the frame. | | |
| 5 | Kites should be made of expensive materials. | | |
| 6 | A fishing line can be dangerous. | | |
| 7 | You should stand at the top of a hill to fly the kite. | | |
| 8 | Kite flying can be done by one person. | | |
| 9 | You have to be fit to fly a kite. | | |
| 10 | You should watch out for birds. | | |

## **Communication Activity:** Reading passages

If I could do anything I'd be the England football captain and walk out at Wembley in my England shirt. It would be the best day of my life.
Jason 7

I'd like to learn how to fish. Then I could go with my brother and father on Sundays. Instead I have to stay behind with my mother and do drawing.
Sally 4

If I were the greatest athlete in the world I'd go round all the hospitals with children in to cheer them up and I'd let them touch my medals.
Leroy 6

I'd go to Russia if my mother would let me and learn to be a gymnast. It'd be a dream come true.
Kelly 12

## **Use of English:** Paragraph writing

Using the information in the passage below, complete the four paragraphs, giving reasons for your choice.

Have you ever thought of taking up a new hobby, or maybe improving your school French, or even learning how to repair and maintain your own car? Perhaps you think you haven't got enough time or that it costs too much money to do these things. Well, you wouldn't have to spend too much time or money if you went to a local Adult Education class, where you'd find similar people to yourself enjoying themselves and learning something new at the same time. And each class is under two hours long and there are less than 30 per 12 week course.

If you are interested in sport, we have badminton for beginners on Monday evenings at 6.30, skiing on a dry ski slope on Tuesdays at the same time. There's keep fit for the over 50s on Thursday at 8.00 or yoga on Monday evenings at 9.

Those of you interested in cooking might like Oriental Cuisine classes, Tuesday at 7.00, and to make sure those of you on your own don't miss out on good food, how about Cooking for One at the same time on Wednesdays? For our experts there are the regular lunchtime sessions on Tuesdays and Thursdays for Entertaining with Food.

Have you let your foreign languages get rusty? Well, every night at 7.00 there's a class for you. We start the week with Italian on Mondays, then it's Greek, French, German and finally Spanish on Friday – that's a different part of the world to discover every night. And if you are going abroad you might like our wine appreciation classes on Wednesdays at 6.00, or how about bringing back a real souvenir – learn to draw on Friday mornings at 10.00 and send your friends back a sketch of the beach.

For the mechanically minded there's Car Maintenance at 6.30 on Wednesdays and DIY

on Tuesdays at 8.00. Those people wishing to prepare for the future or just understand their children might like to try their hand at computing and word processing on Fridays at 12.00.

That's just a selection of our classes so why not come into your local library or leisure centre and pick up a new brochure? But hurry! You'd better be quick because our classes are always popular!

Janet Brown (37) has just moved to Newtown and is thinking of taking some evening classes as a way of meeting new people. As she works as a lecturer she cannot start any classes before 7.00 except on Fridays when she has a day off. She's always enjoyed travelling and would like to go to Italy next year. She lives on her own and likes to keep fit. At school she played tennis and badminton. She doesn't drive and hates anything to do with machines.

Now complete the paragraphs.

**1** The classes I would recommend most for Janet Brown are ..........................................

..................................................................

..................................................................

..................................................................

..................................................................

**2** I think she might be interested in .................

..................................................................

..................................................................

..................................................................

..................................................................

..................................................................

**3** I don't think she would be interested in ........

..................................................................

..................................................................

..................................................................

..................................................................

..................................................................

**4** She definitely wouldn't be interested in ........

..................................................................

..................................................................

..................................................................

..................................................................

..................................................................

## **Communication Activity:** Asking for information

**1** When we are asking a stranger for information we want to sound polite. We don't ask a direct question, instead we disguise it.

Look at these examples:

Direct: How much does it cost?
Polite: Can you tell me how much it costs?

Direct: What time does the pool open?
Polite: Could you tell me what time the pool opens, please?

Direct: Is there a changing room?
Polite: I wonder if you could tell me if there is a changing room.

What changes are made to the direct question?

**Exercise**

Make these questions sound more polite:

**1** How often do you play tennis?
**2** Where is the nearest tennis court?
**3** What time does the match start?
**4** How much is this racquet?
**5** How many lessons do I need?
**6** Is there an empty court?
**7** Can I join now?
**8** Do you have classes for beginners?

# Progress Test 2

## Paper 1: Reading comprehension

### Section A

In this section you must choose the word or phrase which best completes each sentence.

**1** Fairley Motors ...... their latest sports car at the London Show.
A exhibited B explained
C examined D entranced

**2** I think I should buy a new ...... for the wedding.
A costume B clothes C outfit
D clothing

**3** Let's go for a drive in the ......
A environment B countryside
C neighbourhood D surroundings

**4** That jacket really ...... your dress.
A matches B suits C agrees D fits

**5** He fell down the stairs and was lucky to receive only a nasty black ......
A cut B injury C wound D bruise

**6** Although it is ...... expensive, London is cheaper than Paris.
A quite B even C absolutely D just

**7** My sister had a baby yesterday, and she is my first ......
A nephew B cousin C niece D relation

**8** Mr Hedge refused to take part in a televised debate with his ......
A competitor B opponent C enemy
D contestant

**9** He looked ...... the room and smiled at me.
A across B through C past D along

**10** The old man was very angry when the girl came and stood ...... him in the queue.
A in front of B opposite C facing
D beside

**11** The teacher asked the class to draw the ...... of their favourite animal.
A shape B form C size D figure

**12** The package was too heavy for him to ...... across the road
A hold B carry C wear D grip

**13** We stopped for a rest ...... the middle of the field.
A on B in C at D by

**14** The baby was frightened ...... the sound of the dog.
A with B in C from D by

**15** Have you seen Giorgio's latest ...... for evening dresses?
A plans B schemes C portraits
D designs

**16** George has ...... the new head of leisure services in Brighton.
A received B become C got
D obtained

**17** The room was filled ...... people and the meeting began.
A by B with C of D in

**18** I'm thinking of taking ...... badminton to get fitter.
A in B over C up D on

**19** If you look ...... your left you'll see the Alps.
A at B on C to D into

**20** Using a ...... name on your passport is a criminal offence.
A wrong B incorrect C evil D false

**21** My wife is the only daughter in a large family so I have many ......
A brothers-in-law B brothers-in-laws
C brother-in-laws D brethren-in-law

**22** By ...... there was one seat left for the evening performance.
A luck B fortune C opportunity
D chance

**23** She ...... her finger to her lips for silence.
A raised B rose C extended D increased

**24** Walking through town she came ...... an interesting bookshop.
A over B on C across D round

**25** You'll get ill ...... you stop working so hard.
A until B when C unless D if

## Section B

After each of the passages in this section you will find a number of questions or unfinished statements about the passage, each with four suggested answers or ways of finishing. You must choose the one which you think fits best. Give one answer only to each question. Read each passage right through before choosing your answers.

### Passage 1

The traveller slipping southward along the heel of Italy as if down a Christmas stocking full of small treasures and expected gifts first feels the presence of the border a long time before he reaches the port of Brindisi.

Already the wilder southern parts have been replaced by a collection of charming green counties – Manfredonia and its threatening-looking group of headlands falls away to the left. And by now evening is falling too with its greenish exhausted spring lights. Our traveller is wise to choose spring for the journey he has in mind. It is a long way down the stocking of Italy and night is beginning to overtake him. Whether by car or by train it is the same. He empties the last of his wine and eats his last sandwich. Brindisi will provide him with both and if he is a motorist it will also provide him with a comfortable ferry for the night journey. The little town marks the frontier. Beyond it the Greek islands waiting for him out there in the darkness. What will they be like?

What gives a frontier its magic? Not the territorial or political boundary because these are artificial. A sudden change of scenery may be responsible but often the change of country is not accompanied by any change of flora or fauna. Perhaps it is the language that gives crossing a frontier its definite flavour of a voyage. Whatever the answer the magic is there. Everything will seem changed, including the air he breathes. In Greece it is . . . But let us not anticipate.

**1** To reach Brindisi the traveller
A should wear good shoes.
B must be prepared to buy presents.
C travels south.
D must see the port first.

**2** The traveller arrives in Brindisi
A as night falls.
B as the lights go out.
C as spring comes.
D as he runs out of food and drink.

**3** The traveller can
A buy provisions in Brindisi.
B see the Greek islands in the dark.
C spend a day in Brindisi.
D get to the border with Greece.

**4** What always makes a frontier so special?
A The language has changed.
B There is a different form of government.
C The countryside does not alter.
D The feeling of difference.

**5** The writer seems to be
A frightened.
B excited.
C confused.
D amused.

### Passage 2

## Ski Clothing

**Ski Pants**

These should be made of snow-proof material which also allows maximum movement. Ordinary jeans are not recommended as they quickly get wet and become uncomfortable to wear.

**Overtrousers**

A good investment as they are very warm and washable. They can be bought separately or as part of a ski suit. Usually they have zips so they are easy to put on.

**Anorak**

An essential item which should be light and snow-proof. Make sure you have enough room for a thick sweater under it.

**Gloves**

Always wear gloves to keep your hands warm. The best ski gloves are made of leather and they too should be big enough to wear another pair of woollen ones underneath.

**Headgear**

Always have a woolly hat. A warm head is more important than warm hands or feet. Make sure it covers your ears.

**Ski socks**

The best sort are the two-in-one variety with a woollen inside and a nylon layer on the outside.

**Sweaters**

Two or more thin sweaters are warmer than one thick one. In fine weather a thick sweater is as good as an anorak.

**Ski bag**

This is useful for carrying money and other items. The best ones are fixed to your belt.

**Sunglasses**

These are essential because of the brightness of the snow. It is very uncomfortable and dangerous to ski without protecting your eyes. There are different colours for the various conditions.

**Sun cream**

Always protect your face and use lip salve to stop your lips from becoming too dry.

**1** When skiing it is advisable to wear
- A two pairs of trousers.
- B ordinary jeans.
- C tight water-proof trousers.
- D loose water-proof trousers.

**2** You must wear
- A a warm hat.
- B leather gloves.
- C two pairs of gloves.
- D a thick anorak.

**3** The writer says that for socks
- A wool is warmer than nylon.
- B nylon is warmer than wool.
- C you should choose a natural inside and an artificial outside.
- D you should choose an artificial inside and a natural outside.

**4** Which of these statements is true according to the text?
- A A jacket is always necessary.
- B Nothing is warmer than an anorak.
- C A sweater can replace an anorak.
- D An anorak is not as warm as a sweater.

**5** You must
- A protect your eyes from the snow.
- B protect your eyes from the strong light.
- C protect your face from the snow.
- D protect your lips from the strong light.

## Passage 3

A In 'Kingdom of Light' Robert Blanchard has produced a memorable account of war seen through the eyes of a child. His disturbing experiences of death camps and forced marches show us a vision of the world we don't want to let happen again.

B In this first volume of her extraordinary autobiography Mary Angeles beautifully describes her childhood in the American South of the 1930s. She and her brother live with their grandmother in Stamps, Arkansas. She discovers the pleasure of dance and theatre and the dangers of the innocent trust of strangers.

C Fired by a fascination with trains from his earliest years, Peter Thompson sets out one morning with the intention of getting on every train that departed from Victoria Railway Station in London. His travels eventually take him from Tokyo, Japan to Bombay in India but this is a travel book with more than one difference: a fascinating journey which the author undertakes purely for pleasure and a sense of discovery and adventure. One of the most entertaining books you will read this year.

D Mrs Eliza Braddock wanted a nice clean private detective who didn't smoke or drink and wanted $1000 very badly. Badly enough to help her find her lost son. What she didn't mention was that her son probably didn't want his mother to find him. Still Monroe needed the money and he certainly wasn't afraid of using all his skills to find the son and claim that money. Even if his skills made the Police Department a little nervous sometimes. What he didn't know was that he wasn't the only one who was looking for the Braddock boy but he was the only one interested in finding him alive.

**1** Three of the books
- A have a child as the hero.
- B are about children.
- C are about war.
- D are about travel.

**2** In two of the books
- A a child has a difficult time.
- B a child loses his parents.
- C a child enters the world of entertainment.
- D a child is found dead.

**3** The book described in C is about
- A trains.
- B stations.
- C journeys.
- D entertainment.

**4** The book described in D is probably
- A sad.
- B frightening.
- C interesting.
- D complicated.

**5** Which of these statements is true?
- A The first book is a comedy.
- B The subject of the second book is the author.
- C The third book is an adventure book.
- D The fourth book is about money.

## **Paper 5:** Interview

**1** Talk about this photograph. Then take part in one of the Interview exercises which will be given to you by your teacher.

Task: Using the information given decide what a family living in the south west of England might decide to do this weekend. Here are some possibilities to help you (but you may use any ideas of your own that you think are suitable):

pony trekking

go shopping

visit the open air museum

spend a day at the seaside

stay with relatives in Wales

**FORECAST: Cloud with occasional light rain will cover much of central, southern and south-eastern England as well as Wales while isolated showers continue near the northeastern coasts. The west and northwest will have variable amounts of cloud with long sunny spells. The winds will remain east or north easterly fresh at times in the south but light or variable in the north later. Staying mild with temperatures on the cool side in the south. OUTLOOK: Unsettled and showery in the south and east with increasing cloud and the chance of rain in the far north-west during Wednesday.**

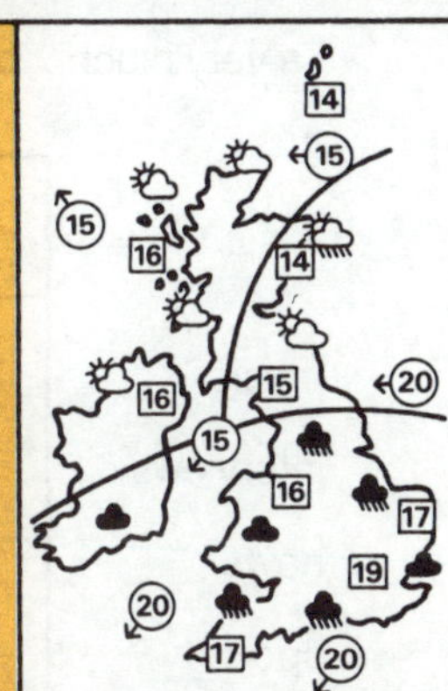

UNIT 7

# Entertainment

## Communication Activity: So do I – Neither do I

Using the questionnaire below, see how many similarities you have with your partner.

**1** Which radio stations do you listen to and how often? Fill in about yourself, then ask a partner. Leave Radio interviewee blank.

**a** often **b** sometimes **c** rarely **d** never

| | You | Your partner | Radio interviewee |
|---|---|---|---|
| Radio 1 | | | often |
| Radio 2 | | | never |
| Radio 3 | | | rarely |
| Radio 4 | | | sometimes |
| Local radio | | | never |
| Commercial radio | | | " |
| Other | | | " |

**2** What sort of programmes do you like and how much? Again, ask a partner.

**a** very much **b** quite **c** not much **d** not at all

| | You | Your partner | Radio interviewee |
|---|---|---|---|
| music | | | v. much |
| interviews | | | " |
| news | | | " |
| sport | | | not at all |

**3** What type of music do you like, and how much?

**a** very much **b** quite **c** not much **d** not at all

| | You | Your partner | Radio interviewee |
|---|---|---|---|
| pop | | | v. much |
| classical | | | quite |
| religious | | | " |
| jazz | | | not at all |
| folk | | | " |
| other | | | — |

**4** Do you own any of these?

| | You | Your partner | Radio interviewee |
|---|---|---|---|
| radio | | | |
| record player | | | |
| CD player | | | |
| cassette deck | | | |
| other | | | |

**5** Can you play any of these musical instruments?

| | You | Your partner | Radio interviewee |
|---|---|---|---|
| piano | | | |
| guitar | | | |
| drums | | | |
| violin | | | |

**6** Personal information

| | You | Your partner | Radio interviewee |
|---|---|---|---|
| **a** Name: | | | |

| | You | Your partner | Radio interviewee |
|---|---|---|---|
| **b** House owner | | | |
| Tenant | | | |
| Lodger | | | |
| Other | | | |

| | You | Your partner | Radio interviewee |
|---|---|---|---|
| **c** –16 | | | |
| 16–25 | | | |
| 25–40 | | | |
| 40–60 | | | |
| 60+ | | | |

## **Listening:** Listening habits

A market researcher is interviewing someone about their listening habits.

Complete the information from the interview onto the questionnaire above, under the heading Radio Interviewee.

## **Use of English:** Paragraph writing

Look at the following Entertainments page from the local newspaper.

Using the information you have found out about David Small from the Listening Survey (Listening Habits, p. 69), choose what you think he would like to do, would quite like to do and would not enjoy at all.

Complete the paragraphs giving reasons for your recommendations in about 50 words each.

Paragraph 1: I would recommend that David Small

Paragraph 2: I think he might also enjoy

Paragraph 3: I don't think he'd like

Paragraph 4: I definitely do not recommend

**Cannon Cinemas:** Next week for 7 days:
Cannon 1: *Good Morning Vietnam* – the DJ who brought pop to the troops.
Cannon 2: *Bird*, the life and times of a jazz legend.
Cannon 3: *A World Apart*, the private and public life of a reporter in South Africa.

**University Hall:** Tuesday 8.00 – *Betty Carter*, finest living US jazz singer, with own band.
Friday 8.00 – *Metalmouth* Loud!

**Warehouse Theatre:** Wed–Sat, 7.30 *Headlines*, press drama!!

**Meeting House:** Friday 8.30 – *Richard Owens*, guitarist and singer of traditional songs.

**College Chapel** – *St John's Church Choir* sing sacred music from all over the world. Open to members of all faiths. Free admission.

**Palace:** Thursday, 7.30. *Buy Me!!!* Lecture on TV ads by C. Brinkley.

**Civic Centre:** Tues., 7.30, *Bananarama!* UK No. 1 band play their TOP 20 hits!! Wed., 8.00, *Royal Orchestra*, under Sir Cyril Foot, play classical melodies from 19th century.

**Odeon Cinemas:** For 7 days – Odeon 1: *Country Girl* – life in Wales 100 years ago – real old songs and dance.
Odeon 2: *World Cup 86* – all the goals and action from Mexico, including the Final.

**Stateside Bar** – enjoy real US food as we play real US Texan country music!!!!

## Reading:
World music

In the mid nineteen eighties disc jockeys in Europe and America were looking as always for new records to play for their audiences. Punk music had come and gone and it seemed people were becoming bored with many musicians' obsession with computerised and synthesised sounds.

By the end of the eighties the DJs had introduced their audiences to literally a whole new world of music that came from almost every continent. They had been encouraged by the success of the Live Aid concert in 1985 when it appeared that virtually the whole world was connected by TV and satellite to watch a concert organised to publicise the suffering of the peoples of Sudan and Ethiopia. It had introduced many people to styles of music from all over the world as musicians from America, Asia, Africa and Europe gave their services free to play in London and Philadelphia. Few listeners knew what the words of the songs meant or could even pronounce the names of the bands properly but what they did like was the energy and vitality of the music, which seemed so different from what they had been listening to in the past.

Many people had not realised how exciting traditional music from other countries was. It was uncommon for American or British radio stations to play any songs that were not written in English and even music from places like Australia and Canada was not considered to be popular enough for the mass market. As many of the so-called world musicians who had come to Europe and the States were often concerned to educate their audiences about the conditions in their native land their songs were regarded as too political and only of interest to a minority of listeners.

The breakthrough came when DJs realised that, whether or not the audience understood or cared about the message in the music, it was music that people liked and wanted to hear more of. It had become fashionable to discover a new style and to be the first to introduce it to the listening public.

Of course when they talked about world music they were talking about a great variety of music from many different areas. While the first styles to get attention naturally came from countries like South Africa and Ethiopia interest quickly spread to other parts of the world. Increasingly too, the Western audiences were introduced to a fusion of their own pop music and more traditional styles. It was a curious twist of history. Much of modern Western music had been derived from the songs of the African slaves who had been taken to America 200 years before and now the African musicians were borrowing the music back.

Multiple choice: choose the answer which best completes the sentences.

**1** In 1988 disc jockeys
**a** did not play punk music.
**b** had discovered new styles of music to play.
**c** organised a concert about Africa.
**d** played to audiences from all over the world.

**2** The new music
**a** had unpronounceable words.
**b** was listened to by a few people.
**c** had been written since 1985.
**d** was played by people from different continents.

**3** Political songs
**a** were not popular.
**b** were only listened to in Australia and Canada.
**c** were not written in English.
**d** were written about education.

**4** World music was taken up by DJs because
**a** they wanted to educate their listeners.
**b** listeners enjoyed the exciting rhythms.
**c** it was fashionable.
**d** they were bored with English songs.

**5** World music
**a** was first played in Africa.
**b** is often a mixture of styles.
**c** was sung by slaves.
**d** is less than 200 years old.

## Word Search

Find words or phrases in the text that mean the same as the following:

**a** presenter of popular music on the radio
**b** uninterested in
**c** not naturally produced
**d** given confidence by
**e** very nearly
**f** smaller number than half of a group

## Writing: Narrative

This kind of exercise will help you in writing a narrative.

Which of these sentences does the picture illustrate?

**1** **a** They left the hall when the fire broke out.
**b** They were leaving the hall when the fire broke out.
**c** They had left the hall when the fire broke out.

**2** **a** The pop star crossed the road when he saw the fans.

**b** The pop star was crossing the road when he saw the fans.

**c** The pop star had crossed the road when he saw the fans.

**3** **a** At nine o'clock the concert started.

**b** At nine o'clock the concert was starting.

**c** At nine o'clock the concert had started.

**4** **a** When the critic arrived at the hall the musicians left.

**b** When the critic arrived at the hall the musicians were leaving.

**c** When the critic arrived at the hall the musicians had left.

## **Writing:** Narrative

Put the verbs in the passage in the correct tenses. (*Past Simple*, *Past Progressive*, *Past Perfect*)

### A Birthday Surprise!

Jim and Katie (1. live) in the country so they (2. not go out) often, in the evenings. However it (3. be) Katie's birthday last Saturday and Jim (4. spend) Thursday and Friday arranging a surprise. He (5. telephone) all their friends and (6. ask) them to meet him and Katie at her favourite restaurant.

On Saturday evening Jim (7. tell) Katie to get dressed ready to go out. Katie still (8. not know) about Jim's idea. When they (9. be) ready they (10. get into) the car and (11. begin) to drive into the nearest town. Katie (12. sit) next to Jim and (13. ask) him where they (14. go) but Jim (15. refuse) to tell her.

While they (16. drive) through the countryside they suddenly (17. hear) a loud noise. They (18. stop) as soon as they (19. can). When they (20. park) at the side of the road they (21. get out) and (22. look) at the car. They (23. have) a puncture. They (24. start) to change the tyre but as they (25. replace) the old one it (26. begin) to rain! Katie and Jim (27. wear) their smartest clothes but now they (28. be covered) in mud and grease from the car.

By the time they (29. finish) but they (30. be) so tired that they (31. not want) to go out so they (32. go) home and (33. telephone) the restaurant. When they (34. hear), their friends (35. decide) to come over and cook them a meal at home instead!!

## **Communication Activity:** World music tour interview

Due to unprecedented interest in 'world music' a record company has arranged a nationwide tour by several of the world's most popular musicians. As they arrive at the airport they are met by reporters from the daily and music papers.

The musicians agree to hold a press conference.

Students A – The Group

Decide:

- what music you play
- what instruments you play
- how you started as a musician
- what the group has done
- your future plans

Students B – The Managers

Decide:

- how the tour was organised
- when you met the members of the group
- what the plan for the tour is

Students C – The Reporters

Decide:

- what kind of newspaper you work for
- what your readers would like to know about the group
- what questions you will ask the members of the group

## **Use of English:** Incomplete dialogue

Dick Ashley, a well-known British pop star, has been asked to talk about his early days in the music business.

Complete the dialogue by writing out the interviewer's questions.

**1** You: ............................................................?
Ashley: Well it was lucky really. I was working as an engineer in the studio when one day we had nothing to do so I asked if I could try out one of my songs and we recorded it then.

**2** You: ............................................................?
Ashley: I'd played in front of friends and at parties but never anything serious.

**3** You: ............................................................?
Ashley: Pete Johnson of PJR records heard it and liked it so much, he offered me a recording contract to make an LP.

**4** You: ............................................................?
Ashley: Oh yes, it's hard work but I really like being in front of so many people having a good time.

**5** You: ............................................................?
Ashley: I've made four albums so far and I'm working on my latest one at the moment.

**6** You: ............................................................?
Ashley: About two months so far, which is a long time but I want it to be my best yet.

**7** You: ............................................................?
Ashley: Well, hopefully I'll be able to keep on doing what I enjoy most, which is singing and performing.

**8** You: ............................................................?
Ashley: Thank you very much.

## **Communication Activity:** Poetry can be fun

In the 1960s poetry came down from the dusty shelves to the ordinary person in the street. The Liverpool poets wrote poetry that everyone could understand and read them to audiences in clubs and bars, sometimes to musical accompaniment.

You too can write poetry!

TONIGHT AT NOON, a love poem by Adrian Henri, was inspired by a jazz piece of the same name, by Charles Mingus. Looking at the title, it seems that Adrian Henri is using nonsensical ideas. How can noon be at night time? Think about the images in the poem and see if you can guess what the missing words are. The first one is done for you.

TONIGHT AT NOON

Tonight at noon
Supermarkets will advertise 3d (1)extra on everything
Tonight at noon
Children from (2).......... families will be sent to live in a home
Elephants will tell each other human jokes
America will declare (3).......... on Russia
World War I generals will sell poppies in the streets on November 11th
The first daffodils of (4).......... will appear
When the leaves fall (5).......... to the trees.

Tonight at noon
Pigeons will hunt (6).......... through the city backyards
Hitler will tell us to fight on the beaches and on the landing fields
A tunnel full of (7).......... will be built under Liverpool
Pigs will be sighted flying in formation over Woolton
And Nelson will not only get his eye back but his (8).......... as well
(9).......... America will demonstrate for equal rights in front of the (10).......... House
And the Monster has just created Dr (11)..........

Girls in bikinis are (12).......... bathing
Folksongs are being sung by real folk
Art galleries are closed to people over 21
Poets get their poems in the Top (13)..........
(14).......... are elected to insane asylums
There's jobs for everyone and nobody (15).......... them
In back alleys everywhere teenage lovers are kissing in broad daylight
In forgotten graveyards everywhere the dead will quietly bury the (16)..........
and
You will tell me you (17).......... me
Tonight at noon

UNIT 8

# Heritage

## Communication Activity: Past and present

Look at these pictures.

In what ways do they show a world different from today?

Discuss with a partner.

22 A Timber-framed House
*Drawing founded on Rumwood Court, Langley, Kent*

## Reading: The first Elizabethan Age

In Great Britain we often mark our historical periods by naming them after the current king or queen.

Thus we had the Victorian period and now we are in the Elizabethan time of our present queen. However, as her name suggests, Elizabeth II has a predecessor, Elizabeth I, who was Queen of England from 1558 to 1603.

Both periods can be described as times of change for the country ruled over by a well-liked and respected Queen. However, 400 years ago this island looked very different.

To modern eyes the 16th century countryside would seem empty, even though 90% of the population used to live outside the towns. London, the capital city then as now, had a population of a mere 60,000 people. Compare that to the 8 million today. There were only another half dozen or so cities in a land of small villages which were many miles apart.

In the 1500s there was a stricter division of society from the nobility at the top down through the rich farmers and merchants to the working population of peasants, labourers and craftsmen and the gap between the highest and lowest was even greater than today. Unlike today it was also possible to tell someone's position by the styles and colours of their clothing. In fact a law was passed which prohibited labourers from wearing clothes that were not brown, blue or tawny.

For most people life was both harder and shorter then. Only 1 in 10 Elizabethans used to reach the age of 40, whereas today most British men and women can hope to live past their 70th birthday. The infant mortality rate was extremely high, with 8 out of 9 babies dying before their fifth birthday.

Parents therefore had as many children as possible in the hope that some would survive to become adults. Consequently, families with 12 or 13 offspring were not unusual.

In the 16th century everyone had to work unless they were very wealthy, and education was not for all. Although some poorer children could go to village schools, at important times like the gathering of the harvest everyone had to work in the fields. At the grammar schools for the sons of prosperous families the lessons were very different from today. A pupil 400 years ago used to learn Latin and ancient Greek well enough to speak and also how to speak in public and present a good argument. However, he probably wouldn't have had to take so many examinations!

When the schoolboy returned home it would be to a much simpler house with little furniture and little decoration. The houses were very dark, draughty and cold, with often only a single fire. The most important piece of furniture was the family bed, which used to be handed down through the generations. Many people did not sleep lying down but sat upright surrounded by pillows. Many poorer people did not possess proper beds and would sleep on the floor resting their heads on logs of wood.

Hygiene and health were far worse than today. Taking a bath once a month was thought to be excessive, and the laundry used to be done once every 2 or 3 months. Toilets were a new invention and still far from common. Most people didn't use to visit a doctor, who was considered to be too expensive and often too painful to see. Instead, many people would go to the local wise man or woman to get a herbal cure. Plagues and other contagious diseases were widespread. Even the cosmetics that women used were dangerous. It was a land where few people travelled for pleasure. For most, knowledge of the world outside was limited and indeed many of their ideas resemble superstitions to us nowadays. For example, people would consult an astrologer before making any important decisions, like deciding when to get married. Yet it was also a time for great explorers and discoverers like Sir Walter Raleigh and Sir Francis Drake.

The arts flourished, too. It was the time of Shakespeare and Elizabethan people used to visit the theatre far more than our contemporaries. There were family evenings of songs and dance, and card games were popular too. Outdoors the rich would go hunting and the country folk used to play a very different type of football. Villages used to play as a team and there were many injuries and a great deal of damage as the 'ball' of pigskin was kicked, carried and thrown through the fields towards one or other of the villages.

Most of all it was a time of peace and relative prosperity for a country that had experienced civil war only a hundred years before.

Choose the answer which best completes the sentences.

**1** In the 16th century
**a** most people lived in villages.
**b** the countryside was empty.
**c** London was the largest of six cities.
**d** most people lived outside.

**2** In the 1500s
**a** everyone wore uniforms.
**b** there were more poor people than today.
**c** there were three classes in society.
**d** there was less equality than today.

**3** According to the passage, children
**a** often died very young.
**b** were fatter and shorter than today.
**c** usually grew up with many brothers and sisters.
**d** went to work after their fifth birthday.

**4** Houses
**a** were painted in dark colours.
**b** were not as comfortable as today.
**c** had very small pieces of furniture.
**d** had only a single bed for the family.

**5** Most people
**a** were unhealthy.
**b** travelled to work.
**c** were superstitious.
**d** couldn't afford doctor's fees.

**6** In the Elizabethan Age
**a** there were more theatres than today.
**b** entertainments were public and private.
**c** there were different types of footballs.
**d** each village had a football field.

## **Vocabulary:** Word building

### -ion / -sion / -ation

**1** Can you find nouns in the passage made from the following verbs?

**a** populate
**b** divide
**c** examine
**d** decide
**e** invent
**f** educate

**2** Complete these sentences by using the correct form of the word in brackets:

**1** The final .......... are in June. (examine)

**2** This museum has one of the largest .......... of Impressionist paintings in the world. (collect)

**3** The main .......... to the plan is that the new road will run through an important historical site. (object)

**4** Archaeologists have discovered an old Roman temple and are making .......... of the area in highly specialised submarines. (explore)

**5** Much of the power of the book is lost in .......... (translate)

**6** Problems of .......... have affected our profits this year. (distribute)

**7** During their .......... the police found large sums of money hidden in the cellar. (investigate)

**8** We expect considerable disruption during the .......... to the new digital network. (convert)

**9** .......... to the gallery is to ticket holders only. (admit)

**10** The .......... which destroyed most of the buildings in the area was probably caused by a terrorist bomb. (explode)

## **Listening:** Those were the days

Listen to this conversation in which a grandmother and granddaughter talk about their different experiences.

Then tick whether you think these statements are true or false.

| | | TRUE | FALSE |
|---|---|---|---|
| 1 | Paul wasn't at church today. | T | |
| 2 | The granddaughter is getting married in less than a month's time. | T | |
| 3 | The grandmother hadn't talked to her husband before the wedding day. | | F |
| 4 | The grandfather was a soldier. | T | |
| 5 | The grandmother didn't go to dances. | | F |
| 6 | The grandmother's parents were stricter. | T | |
| 7 | The grandmother approves of her granddaughter's appearance. | | F |

## **Communication Activity:** Whose fault?

**A** Your teacher will give you one sentence from a story. When you are sure you understand it read it out to the rest of the class.

**B** When all the sentences have been heard decide upon the order of the events in the story.

**C** Then decide which of the people in the story are most responsible for the final event that happened. Work with another student to put them in the order of responsibility you think is correct and give your reasons.

## **Reading Comprehension:** Sentence completion

Complete these sentences by choosing ONE of the four possible answers.

**1** The space was too .......... for the car to get through.
**a** thin **b** slim **c** slender **(d)** narrow

**2** Our local literary society is organising a .......... on censorship.
**(a)** debate **b** quarrel **c** argument **d** row

**3** I used to have to do .......... for my grandmother.
**a** tasks **b** works **c** errands **d** commissions

**4** My .......... left for a better position in the USA, just before I joined.
**(a)** predecessor **b** ancestor **c** successor **d** descendant

**5** I .......... up in a poor area of London.
**a** worked **b** brought **c** took **(d)** grew.

**6** The .......... price was higher than I had estimated.
**a** current **b** present **c** actual **d** now

**7** Some people still believe that fairies ..........
**a** survive **b** exist **c** continue
**d** remain

**8** If you tie a .......... on your suitcase it won't get lost.
**a** ticket **b** document **c** label
**d** certificate

**9** The group's world .......... took them to 20 different countries.
**a** tour **b** visit **c** travel **d** voyage

**10** This machine is .......... to very small movements.
**a** sensible **b** fragile **c** sensitive
**d** delicate

**11** The team .......... of three world famous surgeons.
**a** contained **b** consisted **c** entailed
**d** involved

**12** Teachers should .......... their students' confidence.
**a** construct **b** make **c** build **d** create

**13** He .......... success as a writer and critic.
**a** achieved **b** made **c** received
**d** got

**14** This mistake is your .......... responsibility.
**a** unique **b** alone **c** sole **d** lonely

**15** I'm sure you will get .......... of applicants for the post.
**a** enough **b** sufficient **c** plenty
**d** surplus

**16** The old beggar .......... the story of his life.
**a** spoke **b** said **c** told **d** talked

**17** After the lecture the speaker sat down and .......... asked if there were any questions.
**a** then **b** while **c** than **d** to

**18** An actor must learn all his lines by ..........
**a** name **b** himself **c** hand **d** heart

**19** He put the gun out of .......... of the children.
**a** place **b** danger **c** reach **d** control

**20** According .......... the doctor, he'll make a full recovery.
**a** from **b** with **c** to **d** as

**21** You .......... better apologise for your behaviour last night.
**a** would **b** had **c** should **d** must

**22** He was .......... unlucky to be caught.
**a** greatly **b** extremely **c** largely
**d** mainly

**23** I met him once at a party but I haven't seen him ..........
**a** yet **b** still **c** since **d** then

**24** The person .......... whom this is addressed no longer lives here.
**a** at **b** – **c** for **d** to

**25** He studied Latin .......... a child.
**a** during **b** until **c** as **d** for

## **Use of English:** Vocabulary

Each of the following sentences may be completed by TWO or more of these possible answers:

piece item bit sheet part

**a** Is this your only .......... of clothing?

**b** Let me give you a .......... of advice.

**c** The tramp used a .......... of newspaper to keep warm.

**d** They lost every .......... of furniture in the fire.

**e** This is the most overcrowded .......... of the city.

## **Listening:** Guided tour

Listen to the representative of the local Tourist Office taking a group of visitors round a small town called Cranchester and complete the brochure below.

### A BRIEF GUIDE TO CRANCHESTER

from (1).......... century to 20th century.

Cranchester is famous for its castle built (2).......... years ago in local (3)..........

The site for the town was chosen for its (4).......... and (5).......... importance, benefiting from both a (6).......... and a river.

The town's economic prosperity was based on the (7).......... trade, and visitors should not miss the sheep market which is still held every (8)..........

The most well-known historical event occurred on (9).......... October (10).......... when Queen Mary ordered the execution of (11).......... Protestant priests. The Bathshire bank is built on the spot where the (12).......... used to be.

The most unusual building in the town is the (13).......... Its tower was removed by the inhabitants and placed (14).......... the church.

Modern architecture has not left Cranchester untouched. The Council Offices are housed in a controversial building which has won a number of (15)..........

The Leisure Centre has facilities for a number of sports including (16).........., (17).......... and (18)..........

## **Writing:** A talk

You have been asked to give a talk on your town and its historical interest. Write a short description of the town and the features you feel would be of interest to visitors. (120–180 words)

## **Use of English:** Sentence transformation

Rewrite these sentences to mean exactly the same as the ones above.

**1** Many people died young because there wasn't any proper medicine.

If ..................................................................

..................................................................

**2** The Normans built hundreds of castles after the invasion.

Hundreds of castles ....................................

..................................................................

**3** Unless she took her sister she wasn't allowed to go to the dance.

If she ..........................................................

..................................................................

**4** Most goods were transported by water a thousand years ago.

They ............................................................

..................................................................

**5** They used flowers to decorate the town for the carnival.

The town was ...............................................

..................................................................

**6** The reason why the Normans chose Cranchester was because it was on a hill.

If ..................................................................

..................................................................

**7** My grandfather would go to the dance-hall every Saturday night.

My grandfather used ...................................

..................................................................

**8** Nowadays people travel much more than they used to.

People ..........................................................

..................................................................

## **Use of English:** Expanded letter

Make all the changes and alterations necessary to produce, from the following sets of words and phrases, sentences which together make part of a letter.

The first sentence has been done for you.

Dear Hugh,

I / sorry / not write / long time / but / I be / very busy / new job.

Im sorry I haven't written for such a long time...

Last weekend, though, / I go back / my old town / see / some friends.

**1** ..................................................................

..................................................................

I / not go there / many years / and it look / very different.

**2** ..................................................................

..................................................................

If / not see it myself / I not believe it.

**3** ..................................................................

..................................................................

You / remember / town centre?

**4** ..................................................................

..................................................................

There / used / be / beautiful old building / main square.

**5** ..................................................................

..................................................................

They / pull it down / and / build / multi-storey car park.

**6** ..................................................................

..................................................................

I / never see / such / ugly building.

**7** ..................................................................

..................................................................

Whole town / change / so much / I / not find / station.

**8** ..................................................................

..................................................................

If / not ask / policeman / I miss / train home.

**9** ..................................................................

..................................................................

I / glad / not live / there / any more.

**10** ..................................................................

..................................................................

Anyway, I must stop now – it's time I went to bed. I've got an early start in the morning.

Hope to hear from you soon.

Best wishes,

UNIT 9

# Health and Food

## Reading: First Aid

**1** Look at these pictures. Can you describe what is happening?

**2** Now read the following extracts from a guide to FIRST AID and match the texts to the pictures you have just described.

Would you know what to do in an emergency? FIRST AID is an essential skill that can save a person's life in the time it takes to phone the doctor or wait for the ambulance. You might be able to prevent someone from suffering lasting injury. In case you ever need to know, here are some vital techniques.

**A Artificial respiration**

Use when breathing has stopped. With the patient on back, make sure mouth is clear of any blockages. Pinch the nose shut and take a deep breath. Now breathe into the person's mouth. Take your mouth away. Let the patient's chest rise then repeat three times quickly. Continue until expert medical help arrives.

**B Bleeding**

Stop bleeding by pressing hard on the wound to close it. Raise the injured area unless you think the patient has a broken bone. Bandage the wound as tightly as possible. Avoid moving the patient unless necessary.

**C Choking**

Do nothing if the patient is coughing, but if he cannot speak then give four hard blows with your hand between the shoulder blades. If this does not work, put your arms around the victim's waist from behind. Make a fist with one hand and cover it with the other. Now pull your hands inwards and upwards as sharply as possible four times.

**D Electrocution**

Immediately switch off the electricity. Do not touch the victim until you have done this. As a result of electrocution the patient may not be breathing. Apply artificial respiration.

**E Snake bites**

Keep the victim quiet. Wash the wound and wipe it clean. Put on a clean dressing and make sure the victim does not move. Do not suck the wound. Get the patient to hospital as fast as possible.

## Multiple Choice

Circle the correct letter(s)

1 Which passage says you should make sure the person is lying down and does not move? A B C D E

2 Which passage contains the most useful advice if someone has cut themselves badly? A B C D E

3 Which passage contains advice most useful in a restaurant? A B C D E

4 Which TWO passages do NOT mention breathing difficulties? A B C D E

5 Which TWO passages contain advice most useful for people working with machines? A B C D E

## **Vocabulary:** Ill Health

**A** Complete the paragraph using appropriate words from the list below:

surgery
prescription
head
disease
unwell
waiting room
injection
receptionist

examined
ached
fever
infection
swollen
worse
cure
throat

appointment
bandaged
headache
operation
ankle
medicine
temperature
chemist's
neck

I woke up one morning feeling (1).......... My (2).......... was way above normal, I had a nasty (3).......... and a sore (4).........., and my legs (5).......... I phoned the office to explain that I wasn't coming in and then rang the (6).......... to make an (7).......... The (8).......... told me I could have one later in the day. I set off just before midday, wrapped up warmly in a thick coat, with a scarf round my (9).......... As I was getting on the bus, my scarf got caught in the door, nearly strangling me. Getting up from my seat I banged my (10).......... on the ceiling, and as I got off I slipped and twisted my (11).......... I limped into the surgery and was told to sit in the (12).......... Two hours later the doctor (13).......... me but couldn't tell whether my neck was painful and my head was throbbing because of an (14).......... or the injuries received on the bus. He (15).......... my (16).......... foot and wrote out a (17).........., telling me to get the (18).......... from the nearest (19).......... I got home feeling much (20).......... than when I'd left.

Now make sentences with the remaining words.

**B** Here are some multi-part verbs connected with health and medicine. Choose the one which best complete the sentence.

**1** It's good to see him up and about again. He's only just .......... a serious illness.
**a** got over **b** got through **c** got by **d** got across

**2** Jim's not coming into work today. He's .......... a nasty cold.
**a** gone along with **b** gone into **c** gone down with **d** gone under

**3** You've got a bad cough. You should .......... your smoking.
**a** cut off **b** cut down on **c** cut in **d** cut back

**4** It's a dangerous operation but the doctors are confident she'll ..............................
**a** pull over **b** pull round **c** pull through **d** pull to

**5** When the epidemic .......... medical supplies were sent in.
**a** broke down **b** broke in **c** broke up **d** broke out

**6** He's terrified of injections and .......... when he saw the needle.
**a** passed out **b** passed away **c** passed on **d** passed back

**7** He .......... when they splashed his face with water.
**a** came across **b** came off **c** came forward **d** came round

**8** She stayed at home to .......... her parents when they were ill.
**a** look for **b** look out **c** look after **d** look up to

## **Communication Activity:** Asking permission, making requests

**A** Match the pictures to the following dialogues:

**a** *'Would you mind moving to a smaller table?'*
*'Not at all.'*

**b** *'Do you mind not smoking here, please?'*
*'Sorry.'*

**c** *'Do you mind if I take the last slice?'*
*'Go ahead. Be my guest.'*

**d** *'Would you mind if I smoked now?'*
*'I'd rather you didn't.'*

**B** How can the following expressions be used in the situations above?

May I ..........?
Can I ..........?
Do you think I could ..........?
I wonder if you could ..........?
Could you ..........?

**C** Work in groups of three and act out the situations in the cartoons. Use the expressions you have used in A and B.

You are in an exclusive restaurant.

Student A

| You have invited a colleague to lunch. |
|---|

Student B

| You have been invited to lunch by a colleague you don't know very well. |
|---|

Student C

| You are the waiter/waitress. |
|---|

Other ways of asking permission:

| | |
|---|---|
| May I<br>Do you think I could<br>Can I<br>(less formal) | smoke now?<br><br>take the last slice? |

Other ways of making requests:

| | |
|---|---|
| I wonder if you could | move to another table? |
| Could you | not smoke please? |

## **Listening:** About restaurants

Listen to this radio programme about how to get served in a British restaurant and tick whether these statements are True or False:

| | | TRUE | FALSE |
|---|---|---|---|
| **1** | Some restaurants are more relaxed. | | |
| **2** | You need to book your table in advance if you are a vegetarian. | | |
| **3** | The host should arrive first in order to arrange the seating. | | |
| **4** | Guests should let the host talk to the waiters most of the time. | | |
| **5** | Don't forget to order your entire meal at once. | | |
| **6** | You should order what your host is eating. | | |
| **7** | Most countries allow guests first choice of the dishes on the table. | | |
| **8** | Guests should wait until everyone is served. | | |
| **9** | English people do not expect the guest to insist on paying. | | |
| **10** | The person paying for the meal usually leaves the tip. | | |
| **11** | It's considered rude to smoke on your own in most restaurants. | | |
| **12** | Women still expect to be treated differently. | | |

# **Vocabulary:** Food

**A** Can you identify the food in the dishes shown in the pictures?

**B** Preparation.

Which is the odd man out?

Example:

First you wash the ..........
**a** tomatoes **b** lettuce **c** bananas
**d** apples
You wash tomatoes, lettuce and apples, but you don't normally wash bananas!
Answer: **c** is the odd man out.

**1** You peel the ..........
**a** butter **b** apples **c** eggs **d** onions

**2** Then you slice the ..........
**a** spaghetti **b** potatoes **c** bread
**d** mushrooms

**3** Next you grate the ..........
**a** cheese **b** carrots **c** peas **d** onions

**4** After that you chop the ..........
**a** milk **b** pork **c** pineapple **d** beef

**5** Then you pour the .......... into the bowl.
**a** cream **b** butter **c** sauce **d** fish

**C** Equipment and ways of cooking.

Use the following words to label the diagram:

| | | | | | |
|---|---|---|---|---|---|
| **1** | *kettle* | **3** | *frying pan* | **5** | *hot plate* |
| **2** | *oven* | **4** | *grill* | **6** | *saucepan* |

Complete these sentences:

**1** You melt the butter in a ................................
**2** You bake a cake in the ................................
**3** You roast a leg of lamb in the ..........
**4** You fry the onions in a ..........
**5** It takes less time to boil water in a ..........

**D** Quantities
Match the words on the right with the quantities on the left: (some may be used twice)

| | | | |
|---|---|---|---|
| **1** | a litre of | **a** | cake |
| **2** | 10g of | **b** | salt |
| **3** | a kilo of | **c** | oil |
| **4** | a pinch of | **d** | bread |
| **5** | a slice of | **e** | eggs |
| **6** | 2 spoonfuls of | **f** | peas |
| **7** | a loaf of | **g** | flour |
| **8** | a dozen | **h** | honey |

## **Writing:** Writing a recipe

This is part of a letter you received from a friend:

. . . Thank you so much for having us to stay, and for looking after us so well. You must give me the recipe for the dinner you cooked for us on the last evening – it was so delicious . . .

Below is an example answer. Complete the letter by filling in the missing words with the vocabulary you have learnt in Vocabulary: Food.

Dear Hugh,

Thank you very much for your letter. I'm glad you had a good time. You asked me how I made the Spaghetti Bolognaise. I don't follow a recipe but this is how I make it.

To make the sauce you need some olive oil, a large onion, a clove of garlic, three-quarters of a (1).......... of minced beef, a can of tomatoes, a little tomato puree and a (2).......... of mixed herbs. Then of course you need 350 (3).......... of spaghetti, and 50 grams of Parmesan cheese.

To make the sauce, first you (4).......... and (5).......... the onion and garlic. Then you (6).......... them gently in the oil until they're golden. After that, you add the beef to the frying pan, stirring constantly. Then add the tinned tomatoes and tomato puree and season with the (7)..........

Meanwhile, you (8).......... some water in a large (9).........., add the spaghetti and cook for about 12 minutes. When it's ready, drain it, rinse it with fresh water and serve onto the plates. Finally, you (10).......... some of the sauce onto the plates, grate the cheese and sprinkle it on top.

You see, it isn't difficult at all and doesn't take very long.

Hope to see you again soon.

Best wishes,

Jim

## **Communication Activity:** Talking about food

Choose one of the following:
Either

**A** You have been invited to cook a typical dish from your country for an international food fair. With your partner, discuss what you need and how to prepare the meal.

or

**B** You have been asked to talk about the typical diet of your country as well as your own preferences and any specialities you think will be interesting. Prepare the talk with a partner. If he or she is not from your country or region, your talk will compare the different diets.

## **Vocabulary:** Word building

### -ness / -ity

These suffixes can be used to make nouns from adjectives.

**A** What are the nouns for these adjectives?

| sick | ill | anxious |
|---|---|---|
| stupid | lonely | kind |
| scarce | mad | sad |
| safe | great | sincere |
| simple | still | polite |
| weak | real | similar |
| difficult | popular | shy |

**B** Complete these sentences using one of the nouns from the list you have made.

**1** In the interests of .......... we ask all passengers not to smoke during take-off.

**2** Due to the .......... of food during the drought, people had to eat leaves from the trees.

**3** Many inhabitants of big cities suffer from .......... even though they are surrounded by people.

**4** The .......... of the dawn was disturbed by the sounds of the birds as they began to sing.

**5** His .......... caused the accident: he wasn't concentrating.

**6** During her .......... she lost a lot of weight.

**7** She has many strengths, and her only real .......... is her modesty.

**8** It may not seem serious at first sight, but the .......... of the situation is much worse.

**9** I was impressed by his ..........: he seemed to be telling the truth.

**10** I am very grateful for all the .......... you have shown me during this difficult time.

## **Listening:** To jog or not

Look at these statements. Listen to this radio programme about jogging and then mark the statements True or False.

| | Statement | TRUE | FALSE |
|---|---|---|---|
| **1** | Jogging is an expensive sport. | | |
| **2** | A good pair of shoes cost £200. | | |
| **3** | Most people have suitable clothing for running in. | | |
| **4** | If you exercise before you go you won't feel tired. | | |
| **5** | It's easier to jog with other people. | | |
| **6** | Beginners should not try to do too much. | | |
| **7** | You can run at any time of year. | | |
| **8** | Jogging is better at night. | | |

## **Use of English:** Sentence transformation

Complete each of the following sentences so that it is identical in meaning to the finished sentence before it:

**1** I'm sorry I couldn't see you on Saturday.

I apologise ..................................................

**2** We couldn't see the procession because of the crowd.

The crowd prevented ..................................

**3** He failed to answer all the questions.

He didn't ....................................................

**4** Do you mind turning down your radio.

I'd like ......................................................

**5** They've warned us not to go out alone at night.

They've warned us about ............................

**6** He was annoyed because she had parked in front of his driveway.

He objected ................................................

**7** You'd better see a doctor right away.

I advise ......................................................

**8** I am very pleased that your parents will be coming to stay in the summer.

I am looking ...............................................

# Progress Test 3

## Paper 4: Listening comprehension

### Part One

For questions 1–4 write in the missing words from each of these headlines:

**1** Rise in . . . . . . . . . . . . . . . . . . . . for 3rd month.

**2** Narrow . . . . . . . . . . . . . . . . . . . . . for England.

**3** Mysterious . . . . . . . . . seen in London area.

**4** Children . . . . . . . . . . . . by bedtime stories.

For questions 5–16 tick whether you think the statements are true or false.

| | | TRUE | FALSE |
|---|---|---|---|
| **5** | Just under 3 million people are out of work. | | |
| **6** | The government spokesman was surprised because he expected more people to be out of work. | | |
| **7** | Figures have gone up for the third month. | | |
| **8** | If the USSR had scored a goal England would not have qualified. | | |
| **9** | England scored their second goal in the last 15 minutes. | | |
| **10** | The creature appears to be short of food. | | |
| **11** | The creature has not attacked anybody. | | |
| **12** | The report says that the stories have been adapted from their original purpose. | | |
| **13** | Parents should not read their children any stories before they go to bed. | | |
| **14** | It will not snow in the south of the country. | | |
| **15** | The highest temperatures will reach 17 °C. | | |
| **16** | The cold winds will be from the north. | | |

## Part Two

For questions 17–21 fill in the spaces below:

| Radio Highlights Monday 8th January | | | |
|---|---|---|---|
| **Radio ONE** | **Radio TWO** | **Radio THREE** | **Radio FOUR** |
| **7.30**<br>GOOD MORNING with Ivor Nobrane.<br>Non-stop pop news and fun!! | **7.45**<br>NEWS AND WEATHER OUTLOOK with SPORTS REVIEW introduced by Den Watts | | **8.00**<br>NEWS + WEATHER read by James Alexander Gordon |
| | | **8.15**<br>NEWS SUMMARY | . . . (20) . . .<br>WHAT DO YOU THINK? news and current affairs quiz |
| | **9.15**<br>KID'S TIME games quizzes and competitions | **9.00**<br>THEATRE PRESENTATION a new work by A. J. Kingsley | |
| | | **10.00**<br>CONCERT Shubert's . . . (19) . . . with Fiona Soams and the Bally Orchestra led by Alan Craig | **10.00**<br>MORNING SHORT STORY: the last part of 'The Princeling' by M. B. James read by Jo Day |
| **10.30**<br>NEWSLINE | **10.30**<br>. . . (18) . . . presented by Jill Davies and Andy Hill. This week: Your holiday rights | | **10.15**<br>ROUND AND ABOUT. This week we visit . . . (21) . . . Presented by Barry Riley |
| . . . (17) . . .<br>WEATHER BULLETIN | | | |

## Part Three

For question 22 put a tick against the TWO people Jenny describes.

**22**

## Part Four

For questions 23–25 tick ONE of the boxes, A, B, C or D

**23** The man is complaining about

A a broken cassette. ☐

B his bad moods. ☐

C the effectiveness of the tape. ☐

D his job. ☐

**24** The shop assistant suggests

A the tape has worked for thousands of people. ☐

B the customer is not following the instructions properly. ☐

C the customer has hearing difficulties. ☐

D the customer should start up his own business. ☐

**25** The shop assistant seems

A bored. ☐

B angry. ☐

C sympathetic. ☐

D enthusiastic. ☐

**26** Tick what the tape is supposed to help you with. One has been done for you.

| | | | |
|---|---|---|---|
| concentration | ☐ | punctuality | ☐ |
| relaxation | ☐ | dedication | ☐ |
| patience | ☐ | fitness | ☐ |
| memory | ☑ | | |

# Paper 2: Composition

Write TWO of the following compositions. Your answers must follow exactly the instructions given and should be of between 120 and 180 words each:

**1** You have been involved in an accident and will be at home for a few weeks. Write a letter to a friend explaining what has happened.

**2** Write a description of someone you don't like.

**3** What are the advantages and disadvantages of living in a capital city?

**4** A colleague is leaving your office. Write the speech you would make at his or her farewell.

UNIT 10

# *Cinema and The Media*

## **Reading:** Interview with a star

Ask your partner to describe his or her favourite film star.
What qualities do you think an actor or actress should have to be successful in the film world?

In a shabby, rundown gymnasium in a Warsaw neighbourhood two men fight in a boxing ring. One of them is tall and blond and the other short, dark and powerfully built. The shorter man is obviously much stronger and he hits his opponent continually. Finally he turns away. As he does so the younger man strikes out at his back, clearly in anger. The older man faces his young opponent again and hits him hard enough to send him to the floor. As the young man falls, the director shouts 'Cut'.

Actually, I was not in Poland but in France, interviewing Christopher Lambert on the set of his latest film. The scene we had just watched was all the more unusual because he plays the young boxer who turns out to be the priest, Father Popieluszko, whose friendship and support for the Solidarity movement led to his murder by the secret police in 1984.

This film is unusual too in that it represents a new direction for the man who played Tarzan in 'Greystoke', the first of his major film roles. After this beginning and his subsequent roles in 'Subway' and 'Highlander', many people said that Lambert was the new European sex symbol. When I asked him about this he just smiled and said that he never attempted to stop what people thought and that if they were happy then he was happy as well.

We went on to talk about his success as an actor. He said that he didn't think he was doing anything special but that it was a job that he thought was worth doing. However, he thought most of his success had been due to luck. As I talked to him, he seemed to be very level-headed about his career in the film industry. I asked him about his relationship with the public. He did admit that sometimes he found it difficult because he had always been rather shy. However, he added that if people stopped him in the street he thought he should be pleasant to them since it was his fans that had made him a success.

After leaving Geneva, Switzerland, where he had spent his childhood, brought up by his French-speaking parents, Christopher worked as a trainee bank clerk in London, and didn't turn to acting until he was well into his 20s. Although he speaks fluent English, he still has a strong French accent. In fact the only problem he thought he had as a European actor working in an American dominated business was his accent and on the film set there was a voice coach who was trying to help him lose it.

Christopher did not seem much like a film star. When I asked him if he was happy, he said that he loved life in general, but that it had its good sides and its bad sides. He laughed when asked about the future because he knew what he was doing the following year, but no further ahead than that.

As I said goodbye to him I could see the film's director walking impatiently round the set. She shouted directions to the crew in a mixture of French and English. Next to the trailer that was Christopher Lambert's home for the duration of the shoot, a group of French fans were waiting patiently for his autograph. Like him they were quiet and thoughtful. It all seemed rather appropriate.

## Multiple Choice

**1** On the film set there were two men who were
- **a** boxers.
- **b** from Poland.
- **c** of different build.
- **d** angry.

**2** Why is the scene particularly unusual?
- **a** because one of the actors is a priest.
- **b** because one of the actors is knocked out.
- **c** because it takes place in France.
- **d** because a priest is fighting.

**3** Christopher Lambert believes he is successful because
- **a** he has had good fortune.
- **b** he has kept his head.
- **c** he is polite to his fans.
- **d** acting is a worthwhile job.

**4** Christopher Lambert has
- **a** been an actor for 20 years.
- **b** worked in a bank.
- **c** worked in America.
- **d** lost his French accent.

**5** How does the writer describe Lambert?
- **a** strong and quiet.
- **b** dark and thoughtful.
- **c** tall and muscular.
- **d** blond and modest.

## **Use of English:** Sentence transformation

Complete the following sentences to mean the same as the sentence above.

**1** 'You are leaving on tomorrow's flight,' he said.

He said I ......................................................

..................................................................

**2** He said, 'I am starring in a new film.'

He said he ..................................................

..................................................................

**3** She said, 'I enjoyed your latest film.'

..................................................................

She said she ..............................................

..................................................................

**4** The actor told the interviewer, 'I have always played heroes in my films.'

The actor told the interviewer that he ..........

..................................................................

**5** She said, 'I will co-star with Christopher Lambert in Highlander 2.'

She said she ..............................................

..................................................................

**6** She said, 'If we want to see Rambo II this week we must go tomorrow before it finishes.'

She told him that ........................................

..................................................................

**7** They said they had seen that film two years before.

'We ............................................................

..................................................................

**8** She told him they would have won an Oscar if he had taken it more seriously.

'We ............................................................

..................................................................

**9** I said she ought to go to drama school.

'You ..........................................................

..................................................................

**10** He told me his name was Barnaby Barker and that one day I would see it in lights.

'My ............................................................

..................................................................

# **Vocabulary:** Word building

### Exercise 1

## -ship / -hood

Look at these four sentences. In sentences **1a** and **2a** there are two concrete nouns which appear in sentences **1b** and **2b** in slightly different form. How has the meaning of the words changed?

**1a** The **leader** of the expedition talked to the reporters about the team's successful return.

**1b** The newspapers criticised the **leadership** of the Prime Minister during the present crisis.

**2a** The film stars John Boorman's son Charley as a **boy** captured by native Indians.

**2b** The first part of my autobiography deals with my **boyhood** in wartime London.

### Exercise 2

Complete the sentences below with ONE suitable word formed from the word in CAPITALS:

1. The film shows the .......... of two women from very different backgrounds. (FRIEND)
2. The Daily News has published a story about the Vice President's .......... with his secretary. (RELATION)
3. His new novel portrays the .......... between men in wartime. (BROTHER)
4. Entry to the Cinema Club only with proof of .......... (MEMBER)
5. Too many films have a sentimental idea of .......... (CHILD)
6. The government is awarding ten .......... to the School of Drama and Cinema. (SCHOLAR)
7. The documentary exposed the living conditions in the poorest .......... of the city. (NEIGHBOUR)
8. The copyright law exists to protect the .......... of original works of art and literature. (OWNER)

# **Communication Activity:** Scriptwriting

The picture alongside is a scene from a film.

1. Working with your partners, decide who the people are, and what the story of the film is (what happens before this scene, and what happens after it).
   Write a short paragraph describing the plot of the film.
2. Looking at the picture, describe the action in this scene.
3. Now write the dialogue from the scene.

## **Use of English:** Paragraph writing

The passage below is taken from a book giving advice on various careers for school leavers.

Read the passage together with the comments in the margin written by an actor and complete the paragraphs below in about 60 words for each paragraph.

Nonsense, cinema becoming popular again, + more channels = more jobs in future

True – you will often be out of work at first. Good idea to get other training first – part-time work if necessary

Agents are essential – try to get the best (expensive, but worth the money)

### CAREERS ADVICE:

Academic and Vocational Studies.

**Acting**

Prospects for young actors and actresses, however talented, however well trained, however tough and determined, go from bad to much worse. The theatre has been declining for more than forty years and cinema for thirty.

Overcrowding and chronic unemployment in the profession are not new. Equity, the acting union, estimates that the numbers of unemployed actors at any one time vary, but are rarely less than 75%, with an average employment of 17 weeks a year for men, and 12 for women.

Most actors and actresses are dependent on (and must pay a percentage of their earnings to) theatrical agents to provide the link with theatrical managements or television or film companies.

**Qualifications and training**

These three types of institution accept school leavers.

**Drama schools**

Aim to give students complete control over voice and movement, to encourage creativity and flexibility, and teach detailed acting craft skills.

**Specialist drama departments**

in universities, polytechnics and colleges of higher education, treat all aspects of drama, ranging from purely theoretical and historical study of texts right through, in many cases, to practical involvement in play-making – acting, directing, technical aspects, backstage crafts and writing for the stage. Courses vary considerably, though, in the proportion of time they give to performing plays, and some university courses offer little or no practical theatre.

**Drama departments**

Purely academic study of drama generally happens within literary degree courses – in e.g. English, French, German – where the emphasis is usually on textual studies (style, structure, theme) and their relation to the literary and cultural life of the day, some also examining the theatrical setting, but not including any practical drama.

Don't go there straight after leaving school. Get experience in world first...

Not as good as drama schools

Forget it – drama schools much better

The actor agrees with some of the advice and suggestions given in the book.

He thinks ..........................................................

..........................................................

..........................................................

..........................................................

..........................................................

On the other hand, he doesn't agree with all the advice. He thinks ..........................................................

..........................................................

..........................................................

..........................................................

## **Listening:** Hollywood News

Find out from your partner what kind of film he or she enjoys watching most: horror films, westerns, thrillers . . .

Listen to this radio programme, 'Hollywood News', and tick the boxes True or False.

| | | TRUE | FALSE |
|---|---|---|---|
| **1** | 'Hollywood News' is a daily feature of the radio show. | | |
| **2** | Lauretta Limpet says she has information that no-one else knows. | | |
| **3** | The title of Sylvester Stallone's new film is surprising. | | |
| **4** | Sylvester Stallone's co-star is Austrian. | | |
| **5** | Mel Gibson has been working very hard. | | |
| **6** | Lauretta Limpet says she spoke to Mel in a cinema. | | |
| **7** | 'Good Morning, Vietnam' is a documentary. | | |
| **8** | In the Eddie Murphy film, the star works in a restaurant in Africa. | | |
| **9** | Lauretta highly recommends the comedy 'A Fish Called Wanda'. | | |
| **10** | 'Running Man' is a violent film. | | |
| **11** | Lauretta thinks that 'Poltergeist III' is boring. | | |

## **Writing:** Reviews

Critics usually do two things when writing reviews.

They give the readers:

**a** information about the film, play, TV programme or book, and
**b** their impressions and opinions about the work.

Readers can then decide whether or not it interests them.
Like other pieces of writing the review can be organised into paragraphs.

Use the following skeleton plan to write a review of a play, film, book or TV programme. You may use one of the examples given or one of your own choice.

Decide whether or not you want the review to be positive or negative.

Opening paragraph: Information

| | | | | | | |
|---|---|---|---|---|---|---|
| **a** | The book | Shogun | is | set in Japan | in | the 16th century |
| | film | Dr Zhivago | | in Russia | in | the 14th century |
| | play | Romeo & Juliet | was | in Italy | in | the 1980s |
| | programme | Dallas | | in America | at | the beginning of this century |

**b**

| | | | |
|---|---|---|---|
| It was | written | by | Boris Pasternak |
| | produced | | William Shakespeare |
| | directed | | an American TV channel |
| | made | | James Clavell |

**c**

| | |
|---|---|
| It stars | Larry Hagman as one of the brothers |
| Its main characters are | Jane Fonda |
| | Omar Sharif as the doctor |
| | a young girl and boy in Verona |
| | Captain Blackthorn and Toranaga, the Japanese lord |

Paragraph 2: The plot or storyline

**d**

| | | |
|---|---|---|
| The film | depicts | the life of rich oil men |
| book | shows | a tragic love story |
| play | is about | the first Europeans in Japan |
| programme | deals with | the Russian revolution |

**e**

| | | | | | |
|---|---|---|---|---|---|
| It | ends | happily | with the death | of | the main characters |
| | | sadly | marriage | | one of the characters. |
| | | tragically | suicide | | |
| | | mysteriously | disappearance | | |
| | | | triumph | | |

Paragraph 3: Opinion – recommendation/criticism

**f**

| | | | | | |
|---|---|---|---|---|---|
| The photography | was | marvellous | although I | liked | the music |
| writing | is | boring | | disliked | characters |
| acting | | superb | | | beginning |
| | | | | | middle |
| | | | | | ending |

**g**

| | | |
|---|---|---|
| I particularly | admired | the scenes of the Russian countryside |
| | disliked | description of the Japanese customs |
| | | last scene |
| | | ridiculous plot |

**h**

| | | | | | |
|---|---|---|---|---|---|
| I have never | seen | such a(n) | wonderful | film | in my life |
| | read | | awful | book | for years |
| | | | violent | play | |
| | | | superb | programme | |

**i**

| | |
|---|---|
| I would | recommend it to anyone. |
| wouldn't | |

**j**

| | | | |
|---|---|---|---|
| This film | is | well worth | reading |
| book | | not worth | seeing |
| play | | | watching |
| programme | | | |

## **Use of English:** Incomplete dialogue

Look at the advertisements and complete the dialogue below.

> **The perfect gift**
> All your favourite TV programmes on one video.
> Best of British comedies from the year's most popular shows.
> Only **£15.99**

> *Don't go without your*
> **Daily News!**
> 6 months' subscription to your daily newspaper sent anywhere in the world. **£20.**

> Many BBC Radio 4 programmes now available on cassette.
> Phone this number to find out if you can buy a copy of the programme you missed.
> Price depends on length of programme.

> **Food for thought.**
> *A selection of typical English food tastefully presented in a basket and delivered to the door here or abroad.*
> *Normal price: £22*
> *Order now and save £8.*

> Boxed set of 200 classic hits of this decade.
> Every Number One record from the charts, plus more.
> £29.99

Martha: You know Peter's going to the States for 6 months. I thought it would be a nice idea if we got him a present. There are some ideas here.

Martin: Yes, something to remind him of home.

Martha: Shall (1) ................................................

................................................

Martin: Well, I don't think he'll have much time to read while he's over there.

Martha: That's true. Why (2) ................................................

................................................

Martin: I'm not sure if he'll have a video machine where he's staying.

Martha: In that case let's (3) ................................................

................................................

Martin: I'd rather get him something a little less expensive.

Martha: Yes, it is a bit over-priced, isn't it? What

(4) ................................................

................................................

Martin: Brilliant idea. He'll love that.

## **Communication Activity:** Choosing a present

Work in pairs. You want to buy a present for your teacher or someone else in the class. Think about how much you want to spend and what sort of present the person would like. Suggest some ideas to your partner and decide what you are going to buy.

## **Listening:** Planning things to do

Part A

A couple are discussing what to do on their holiday next week. Listen and complete the information on the advertisements below:

COMING SOON TO

**THEATRE ROYAL**

London Royal (5) ..................

Favourite film (6) .................. tunes

(7) .................. evening only

Availability: (8) ..................

---

*Rare chance to see*

**GALEO**

Traditional guitar

(9) .................. from Spain

1 performance only – on

(10) .................., 3 November.

Availability: B

THE DOME

(11) .................. All Stars

---

*Theatre Royal*

(1) ........ (2) ........ Theatre

Ballet company

'The most refreshing thing to Come to the world of dance for

(3) .................., London Times

Mon & Tues

Tickets from £10

Availability: (4) ..................

---

**Circus**

acrobats, clowns, elephants – FUN FOR ALL THE FAMILY

(12) .................. – Sat.

8 p.m. £8–£12

---

**Availability**

A: seats at all prices
B: seats at some prices
C: returns only

## **Writing:** Composition – Discussing alternatives

'TV is a Better Medium than Radio.' Discuss

### Advice on Discursive Composition – (Paper 2)

Sometimes you are asked to compare and contrast two ideas or subjects.

Here you are expected to deal with the relative advantages and disadvantages of the television and the radio.

There are many different ways to plan a composition answer of this type:

**a** you can deal with the two areas separately, giving their advantages and disadvantages in two different paragraphs;

**b** you can deal with the advantages of both in one paragraph, and the drawbacks of both in another paragraph;

**c** you can describe the advantages of A over B in one paragraph, followed by the advantages of B over A in the next paragraph.

Whichever way you choose, you need a clear introduction and conclusion: in this last paragraph you can state your own final opinion, especially if you have strong views on the subject.

Remember to write between 120 and 180 words.

Here are notes for an essay organised according to the third plan.

### Planning notes

Introduction

areas to look at: news/current affairs, entertainment, sport, drama, immediacy, realism, accuracy, interest, cost

Paragraph 2:

Radio – cheap, portable, more adaptable, encourage imagination, intellectually more stimulating

Paragraph 3

TV – visually stimulating, more realistic, additional information from pictures, better made

Conclusion

Prefer radio for thinking programmes, TV for entertainment and programmes where visuals are important

Here are some other titles of compositions involving discussion of two topics.

Choose one with a partner and prepare the planning notes.

1. It is always better to watch a film in a cinema than on TV.
2. You can get more information about current affairs from a newspaper than from the TV.
3. A book can teach you more than any computer.
4. What are the advantages and disadvantages of living in a city and living in the country?

## **Vocabulary:** Definitions

Look at the sentences explaining the meaning of a word:

1. What is a producer?

   Definition:
   A person who/that arranges the finance for a film.

2. What is a trailer?

   Definition:
   A kind of caravan that/which actors live in while on location.
   A short advance publicity film.

3. What is a set?

   Definition:
   A place where a scene is filmed.

## Game

Your teacher will give you some other words.

Write similar definitions.

Now test the other students in the class.

In pairs prepare at least 4 more definitions and ask other students to name the profession, object or place you have defined.

UNIT 11

# Far away places

## **Writing:** Non-defining relative clauses

The following words are used to introduce extra information about people, objects and places:

**who / whose / which / where**

Read the skeleton story below:

---

A LUCKY HOLIDAY / AN UNLUCKY HOLIDAY

We arrived at Simlon Hotel, (1..........), at 11 o'clock at night. The receptionist, (2..........), looked for our names in her book but couldn't find them. There had been some mistake. She called the manager, (3..........), and we went to another hotel, (4..........). The room, (5..........), was on the fourth floor. The next day my husband, (6..........), looked out of the window, (7..........). We rushed down into the street, (8..........).

---

Now expand the story into a lucky *or* unlucky incident using 8 appropriate clauses from the lists alongside:

*Lucky version*

**a** where we had booked a suite for a fortnight
**b** which overlooked the bay
**c** which had a wonderful balcony
**d** who apologised sincerely
**e** who was dressed in a smart uniform
**f** where we saw the burning remains of the first hotel
**g** which he had kindly telephoned for us
**h** who had got up to look at the beautiful weather

*Unlucky version*

**a** which looked nothing like the picture in the brochure
**b** who hadn't slept a wink
**c** which had one last vacancy
**d** where we saw the firemen putting out a blaze in the breakfast room of our hotel
**e** which would not open
**f** who ignored our complaints
**g** who did not seem pleased to see us
**h** which was as small as a cupboard

## **Listening:** Describing places

How much do you know about Australia?

Listen to these people talking about Australia and tick the box marked True or False next to each statement.

| | | TRUE | FALSE |
|---|---|---|---|
| **1** | The state of Western Australia is larger than Europe. | | |
| **2** | The inhabitants of Perth are said to be less reserved than other Australians. | | |
| **3** | Perth is on the coast of the Indian Ocean | | |

4 You can swim in Lake Disappointment.

5 Broome is more lively now.

6 The Northern Territory has a very varied landscape.

7 Only a few tourists can visit the Aborigines on Melville Island.

8 Queensland is popular with Australian tourists.

9 Cairns is north of Cooktown.

10 Rockampton is on the coast.

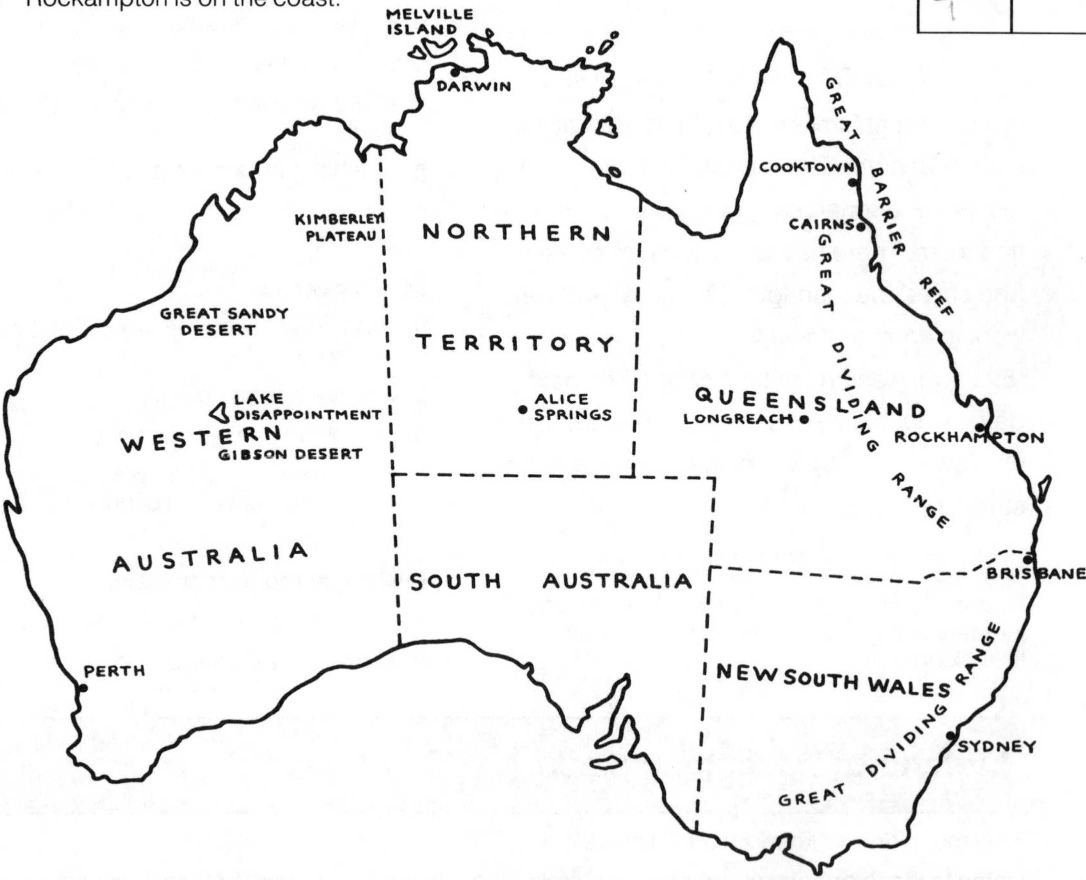


## Advice on the Interview (Paper 5)

Remember: in the Interview part of the examination you are often asked about the country or town where you live. You should be able to describe where it is, what it is like, the climate, the people, how long you've lived there, why you like it/don't like it . . .

Discuss your town or country with a partner.

## **Vocabulary:** Definite and zero article

**the** or ..........?

Look at these places:

Do you recognise any of them?

Work with a partner to put them into the correct columns below:

the Thames, Sydney, the North Sea, Lake Geneva, the Pyrenees, London Road, Fifth Avenue, Panama, the Mediterranean, the Himalayas, Lake Ontario, the River Nile, Rotterdam, New Zealand, the Alps, the Atlantic, the Mississippi, Moscow, East Street, Lake Victoria, Honduras, the Adriatic, Park Lane.

| mountain ranges | rivers | seas/oceans |
|---|---|---|
| | | |

| lakes | towns/cities | street names |
|---|---|---|
| | | |

| countries |
|---|
| |

Write a sentence explaining which of the proper nouns above take 'the' and which do not.

Can you think of any exceptions?

## **Communication Activity:** Maps

Your teacher will give you a map of New Zealand. Students B turn to page 110.

Students A

Ask your partner where these places are on North Island and mark them on your map:

Auckland, Wellington, Great Barrier Island, the Tasman Sea, the Rushine range.

## **Writing:** Composition

Write a short description of a town or area where you would like to live (120–180 words)

## **Reading:** Holiday advertisements

Look at these advertisements.

Which holiday would you choose?

**A**

# 8 NIGHT CARIBBEAN CRUISE. JUST £859

Getting away to a warmer climate is easy this winter with Princess Voyages. For as little as £859 you could be fanning youself in the tropical heat.

From the scent of beautiful orchids in Martinique to the delicious aroma of a barbecue on our private island in the Grenadines, the Caribbean's your oyster.

Dive into a sea of technicolour tropical fish, or change colour on deck. You'll find countless moments to treasure in the Virgin Islands when you visit the land of Bluebeard.

Then return from unspoilt beaches to be completely spoilt on board. After all, no one has more experience than Princess Voyages.

To make sure of your place in the sun this winter, send us the coupon for a free colour brochure, or visit your ABTA travel agent.

*Princess Voyages*

To: Cathy Hadley, Princess Voyages, 107 New Oxford Street, London WC1A 1PP. Telephone: 01 931 2420.

Please send me more information on Princess Voyages to the Caribbean.

Name ..........................................................

Address ......................................................

Postcode .............. Telephone ............

**B**

# RURAL REFUGE

Telephone
037278 434

EXTENDED WEEKEND BREAKS AND MIDWEEK SAVERS

Two special packages to brighten the winter. You can start your weekend break early on Friday and finish late on Sunday – at no extra cost. Come in midweek and we offer you a reduced rate. From cosy cottages for two, to luxurious houses for groups of eight. Whenever you come, Rural Refuge will provide you with delightful old fashioned properties in picturesque Cotswold villages. All are superbly equipped and stylishly furnished, mostly with antiques. A food basket with fine wine will welcome you, and at your request, dinner can be freshly cooked and delivered to your door. Daily and weekly rates available all year.

*Call for a free brochure.*

WELLS FARM, BEXFORD,
GLOUCESTERSHIRE GL56 2XH

**C**

EUROPEAN SAVER

# PARIS

£46.50

5 DAY RETURN FROM LONDON BY RAIL AND SHIP

Ideal for a short break. Fast, comfortable services run from London's Victoria station up to 5 times a day, every day of the week, with connecting services by sea and rail to the centre of Paris. Travel via Newhaven for just £46.50, or take the shorter sea crossing via Dover or Folkestone for just £3 more.

For further details ask for a leaflet from principal British Rail Travel Centres, appointed travel agents, or telephone 01-855 7000. For credit card bookings telephone 01-828 0892.

**Available until 28 February 1990**

**British Rail International**

**D**

AFTER 200 YEARS PERFECTING OUR INDIA BROCHURE, WE'RE STILL OPEN TO SUGGESTION

Our choice of holidays has widened somewhat since 1758. Now every corner of India is forever Cox & Kings.

From the golden sands of Goa to the peaceful Vale of Kashmir, our organised tours cover the length and breadth of India. With that expertise behind you, you can confidently go your own way, backed by 350 local staff (no-one else offers you that kind of service). You can choose special interest tours, go for the wildlife or for the flexibility of a tailor-made package.

Wherever you go, you'll stay in India's finest hotels. Holiday prices range from £725 to £2,000.

So fill in the coupon below and send for our new brochure.

Then make your own suggestions.

**COX & KINGS**

**Services to the traveller since 1758**

Please send me the new Cox & Kings colour brochure on India.
COX & KINGS LTD,
St James Court, Buckingham Gate
London SW1E 6AF

## Multiple-choice Questions

**1** Travelling by sea is part of which holidays?
- **a** A and D
- **b** A and C
- **c** B and C
- **d** C and D

**2** What kinds of activities are mentioned in advertisement A?
- **a** Sunbathing and windsurfing.
- **b** Windsurfing and sailing.
- **c** Walking and flower arranging.
- **d** Swimming and eating.

**3** You can rent one of the cottages in advertisement B
- **a** only at weekends.
- **b** at a cheaper weekend rate.
- **c** only during the winter.
- **d** at any time in the year.

**4** When you buy the European Saver advertised in C you'll get
- **a** a single ticket from London to any town in France.
- **b** a return ticket from England to Paris including meals.
- **c** a train and ferry ticket from London to Paris and back.
- **d** a five-day package holiday in Paris.

**5** Cox and Kings offer the traveller
- **a** a wide range of holidays.
- **b** historical tours of India.
- **c** 350 local guides.
- **d** long tours of India.

## **Communication Activity:** Role play

### A holiday of a lifetime

Students A

> You are travel agents.
>
> You have one excellent holiday left to sell.
>
> Work with your partner and decide.
>
> **1** where it is
>
> **2** what type of holiday it is
>
> **3** what activities/excursions are possible
>
> **4** how much it costs (travel/ accommodation for a fortnight)

Students B

> You are looking for a holiday of a lifetime.
>
> Work with your partner and decide on two possible holidays. Think about:
>
> **1** where you would like to go
>
> **2** what kind of weather you would expect
>
> **3** what activities you would like to do
>
> **4** how much you can afford to spend for a fortnight's dream

## **Use of English:** Paragraph writing

Terry and June, who have never skied before, are booking a skiing holiday in the United States.

Here are their holiday requirements:

Two weeks, from Saturday February 18 to Sunday March 3.

Prefer to try out local restaurants in town.

Short journey from airport to resort.

Look at the details of the two resorts in the brochure illustrated on the next page and complete the two paragraphs below using full sentences.

I think Terry and June will choose to go to ..........

because ............................................................

............................................................

............................................................

............................................................

............................................................

Describe their holiday (price, flight, accommodation etc.)

............................................................

............................................................

............................................................

............................................................

## **Communication Activity:** Maps

Your teacher will give you a map of New Zealand

Students B

> Ask your partner where these places are on South Island and mark them on your map:
>
> Christchurch, Stewart Island, the Pacific Ocean, the Southern Alps, the Tasman Mountains.

# SKIING IN THE USA

## FLIGHT DEPARTURE DETAILS

**UNITED STATES via Denver**

| UK Airport (Flight duration) | Code | Flight days | Departure–Return | |
|---|---|---|---|---|
| GATWICK (12 hrs) | 6498 | Sat | 14.25 | 07.40 (Sun) |
| GATWICK (12 hrs) | 6499 | Thurs | 13.40 | 07.25 (Fri.) |

## BRECKENRIDGE

### Resort Facts

Resort Height: 3200 m
Airport transfer: Denver Airport to resort – 2 hours

### RECOMMENDATIONS

| | |
|---|---|
| Advanced Skiers | *** |
| Intermediate Skiers | **** |
| Beginner Skiers | ***** |

### PRICES PER PERSON

(in £s) include airport charges and flight supplements

| **Hotel & Board Arrangements** | **Breckenridge Inn** | | **Hyways** | |
|---|---|---|---|---|
| | *(Half board)* | | *(Room only)* | |
| Hotel Code | WBB | | WBA | |
| Nights in hotel | 7 | 14 | 7 | 14 |
| Feb 4–Feb 10 | 451 | 580 | 424 | 450 |
| Feb 11–Feb 17 | 468 | 597 | 434 | 480 |
| Feb 18–Feb 24 | 475 | 595 | 450 | 490 |
| Feb 25–Mar 3 | 472 | 601 | 444 | 480 |
| | Shower | | Bath | |

## VAIL

### Resort Facts

Resort Height: 2499 m
Airport transfer: Denver Airport to resort – 3 hours

### RECOMMENDATIONS

| | |
|---|---|
| Advanced Skiers | ***** |
| Intermediate Skiers | *** |
| Beginner Skiers | *** |

### PRICES PER PERSON

(in £s) include airport charges and flight supplements

| **Hotel & Board Arrangements** | **Raintree Inn** *(room only)* | | **Holiday Inn** *(bed & breakfast)* | |
|---|---|---|---|---|
| Hotel Code | WVB | | WBA | |
| Nights in hotel | 7 | 14 | 7 | 14 |
| Feb 4–Feb 10 | 456 | 594 | 513 | 709 |
| Feb 11–Feb 17 | 478 | 616 | 535 | 731 |
| Feb 18–Feb 24 | 481 | 624 | 538 | 739 |
| Feb 25–Mar 3 | 482 | 620 | 539 | 735 |
| | Bath | | Shower | |

## **Use of English:** Expanded letter

Complete this letter by making all the changes necessary.

Dear Sir

**1** Your hotel / recommended / Mr H. Johnson / stay you / many times.

..............................................................................

..............................................................................

**2** He / always / very pleased / your service / hospitality.

..............................................................................

..............................................................................

**3** I / like / make / reservation / myself and wife.

..............................................................................

..............................................................................

**4** We / like / double room / full board / 6 nights / Tuesday 1st / Monday 7th June.

..............................................................................

..............................................................................

**5** We not expect / reach hotel / until / late / Tuesday evening.

..............................................................................

..............................................................................

**6** We / grateful / if / you / provide / meal / when / arrive.

..............................................................................

..............................................................................

**7** Please / also arrange / us / 5-day membership / local golf club.

..............................................................................

..............................................................................

**8** I / gladly send / deposit / when / you / confirm / reservation.

..............................................................................

..............................................................................

Yours faithfully

## **Communication Activity:** Wish you were here

Some people are often not very happy when they go abroad. Here are some of their complaints.

Here are some more:

**7** 'Nobody speaks my language!'

**8** 'It's a pity the beer is so cold.'

**9** 'There's nothing to do in the evenings.'

**10** 'They don't have my favourite TV programmes.'

**11** 'The sand always gets in my sandwiches.'

**12** 'The waiters keep talking to my girlfriend.'

What are they thinking? Use 'I wish . . .' and 'If only . . .'. The first two have been done for you.

**1** I wish it weren't so hot.

**2** If only these people wouldn't make so much noise.

**3** ..........................................................................

**4** ..........................................................................

**5** ..........................................................................

**6** ..........................................................................

**7** ..........................................................................

**8** ..........................................................................

**9** ..........................................................................

**10** ..........................................................................

**11** ..........................................................................

**12** ..........................................................................

## **Vocabulary:** Multi-part verbs

Use these prepositions to complete the multi-part verbs in the text below.

You will have to use some of them more than once.

| | |
|---|---|
| across | down |
| in | into |
| off | on |
| out of | over |
| round | up |

Last weekend my sister was travelling to Germany on business and wanted me to see her set (1).......... at the airport as she's afraid of flying and needs someone there to take her mind off planes. She had to check (2).......... two hours before the plane took (3).......... at midday. We called a taxi to pick us (4).......... at nine o'clock and saw it pull (5).......... outside the house only a little late, at a quarter past. It didn't look like a normal cab. For a start, the passenger door was badly dented. The driver said someone had run (6).......... him the day before. We got (7).......... and set (8).......... for Heathrow. We were chatting to each other when suddenly we felt a bump. We looked (9).......... and saw to our horror that the car had run (10).......... a cat. 'Number three,' said the driver happily. He wouldn't stop and we drove (11).......... in silence. Twenty minutes later we were driving down the approach road to the airport when the engine simply went dead. 'Has it broken (12)..........?' I asked. 'No,' said the driver calmly, 'We've run (13).......... petrol.' Then he explained that he used to be a taxi driver, but that was before the accident. They only let him out of the hospital at weekends. We paid him and got (14).......... the car as quickly as we could. We cut (15).......... the car park taking it in turns to carry the heavy suitcase and made (16).......... the terminal. Saying goodbye at Passport Control, my sister told me that this would be the first time she would feel relieved to get (17).......... the plane. Usually she only relaxed when she got (18)..........

UNIT 12

# Inventors and Inventions

## Vocabulary: Definitions

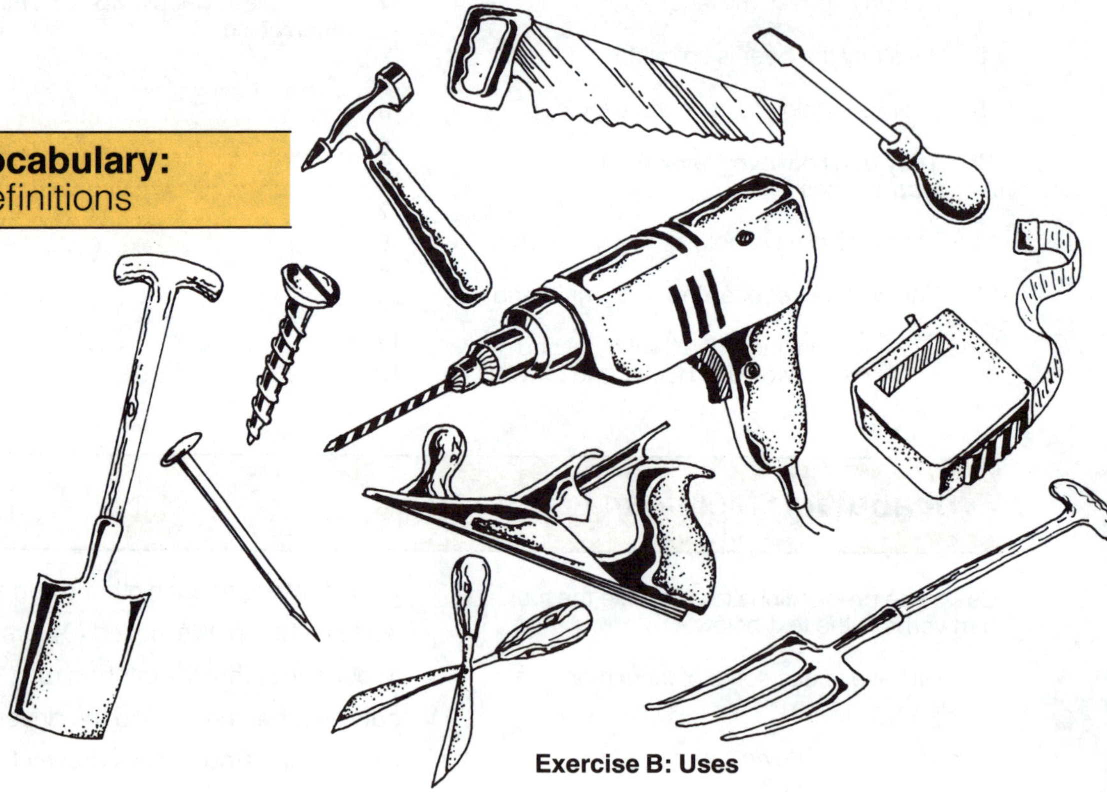

*hammer* | *nail* | *fork*
*screwdriver* | *saw* | *plane*
*drill* | *shears* | *screw*
*spade* | *tape measure*

### Exercise A: Categories

Match the following names of common tools to their appropriate illustrations. Then group them under the following headings: Tools used for:

| Carpentry | Gardening |
|---|---|
| | |

### Exercise B: Uses

Now fill in the sentences with the words in the list above. Each word may only be used ONCE.

**a** To hang a picture you can fix a (1).......... to the wall with a (2)..........

**b** The garden was very overgrown. She had to use both a (3).......... and a (4).......... to dig up some of the weeds.

**c** To hang up the clock he made a hole in the wall with a (5)..........

**d** The piece of wood was too long, so he measured it with a (6).......... and used a (7).......... to cut it in half.

**e** They couldn't see the view from the end of the garden so they got out their (8).......... and cut back the hedge.

**f** The edge of the shelf was very rough so he smoothed it with a (9)..........

**g** To put the wires into a plug you need a (10)..........

### Exercise C: Definitions

When we are describing something we may not always know the correct word, but we can give an idea of what the object is, what it is made of, or what it is used for.

In Exercise A you had to put the tools into categories.

This is one way of describing things:

e.g. A plane is a kind of tool used in carpentry.

In Exercise B you completed sentences about the use of the object:

e.g. A hammer is a sort of tool used to fix nails in walls.

A third possibility is to talk about what the object is made of:

e.g. A nail is a small metal object with a pointed end.

Of course we can combine all three categories in one sentence:

a plane: It's a kind of tool with a metal blade and a wooden handle used in carpentry to smooth wood.

Choose three words from the list of everyday objects below and write a short description of them giving as much information about them as possible.

| | |
|---|---|
| typewriter | seatbelt |
| ladder | tap |
| corkscrew | duster |
| lid | thermometer |
| saucer | shoelace |
| jar | file |
| fridge | toothpaste |
| glue | fan |

### Useful Language

| *It's a(n)* | *made of* | *and is* |
|---|---|---|
| object | metal | used for + ing |
| thing | cloth | used to + inf. |
| device | material | used in + noun |
| machine | wood | |
| instrument | glass | |
| | paper | |
| | china | |

## **Communication Activity:** How does it work?

Your teacher will give you some diagrams.

Student A – look at Diagram 1A.

Be prepared to answer questions on the object.

Think about these categories:
description
size/shape
material
uses

Student B will now ask you about the object

Student B – look at diagram 1B.

It is an object that can be used in the home.

Ask Student A to explain what it is and what it can be used for.

Make questions in the following categories:
description
size/shape
material
uses

Now change roles.

Student B – look at Picture 2A.

Be prepared to answer questions about it.

Think about the following categories:
description
size/shape
material
uses

Student A will ask you to explain what it is and what it can be used for.

Student A – look at Picture 2B.

It is an object used in the home.

Ask Student B to explain what it is and what it can be used for.

Make questions in the following categories:
description
size/shape
material
uses

## Reading: Inventors and inventions

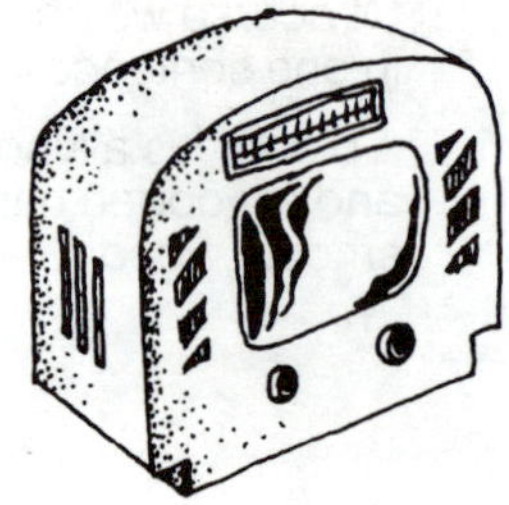

Have you ever stopped to think how many of the everyday things in your life are the product of someone's hard work or imaginative genius? Take this book, for example. It was made by a mechanical printing press that is able to produce large numbers of identical books at great speed. Yet before the German Johan Gutenburg invented movable type in the 15th century all books had to be printed one page at a time, which was very time-consuming and expensive.

What about the electric light bulb you may be using so that you can see the page? It was the work of one of the most prolific inventors of all time – Thomas Alva Edison. An American who registered over 1,000 patents, he was actually expelled from school because of his poor mathematics! Yet he succeeded in becoming very rich through his inventions, which included the first gramophone and that electric light bulb. It was not easy. He had to experiment with thousands of different materials before finding a thread made of cotton which could glow in a vacuum tube.

Sometimes inventions came about by less strenuous methods. Louis Daguerre found out how to make permanent photographic plates when a broken thermometer dripped onto an unsuccessful experiment he had put away in a cupboard. From this lucky accident the first workable photographic process was developed in the 1830s.

Someone else who relied on an accident was the Scot, Alexander Graham Bell. Working in his laboratory on a system to transmit sounds over a long distance, the scientist spilled some battery acid on his trousers. He called out for his assistant who heard him – from the other side of the building – the first words ever transmitted by telephone!

Do you drive a car? Is it a Ford? Even if it isn't the contribution of Henry Ford to our lives is not only the motor car company that carries his name. He also introduced the modern methods of production which mean we can buy the enormous number of consumer goods that are produced in factories all over the world. Whether or not he is well remembered by the men and women who work in them is another question!

Lastly, as you sit at home tonight in front of the television set, ask yourself who invented it. Many people believe a Scot, John Logie Baird, was the inventor, but although he was the first who managed to demonstrate that television was a practical possibility, it was a Russian, Vladimir Zurovykin, who invented the system used by our television sets today. It's not always the right inventor who gets the credit.

**Multiple choice:**

1 Edison invented the light bulb after
  **a** trying out thousands of substances.
  **b** registering thousands of patents.
  **c** creating the first vacuum.
  **d** improving his mathematics.

2 Edison's invention of the light bulb was the result of
  **a** luck.
  **b** hard work.
  **c** necessity.
  **d** ignorance.

3 If Daguerre hadn't kept his unsuccessful experiment
  **a** he wouldn't have had to work so hard.
  **b** he wouldn't have invented photographic plates.
  **c** he wouldn't have broken a thermometer.
  **d** he wouldn't have dropped it.

4 The first words ever transmitted by telephone were probably
  **a** 'Look out, I've spilled some acid!'
  **b** 'I've invented the telephone!'
  **c** 'Quick! Come and help me!'
  **d** 'Alexander, I can hear you!'

5 Henry Ford was the first person to
  **a** work in a factory.
  **b** buy vast quantities of consumer goods.
  **c** drive a car.
  **d** use methods of mass production.

## **Vocabulary:** Cars

Look at these diagrams and label the following parts:

headlights
sidelights
indicator lights
tyre
wheel
exhaust
mirror
steering wheel
windscreen
gear stick
brake
accelerator

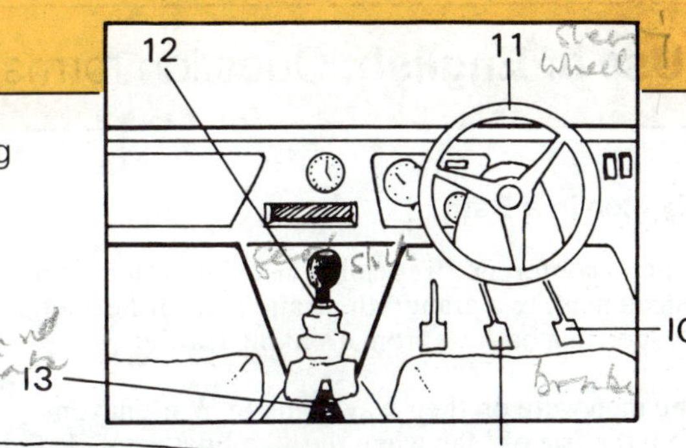

## **Listening:** Traffic offences

Listen to this conversation and complete the police report. Mark with a tick the boxes where the car has faults or where the owner is at fault.

### POLICE REPORT

| Faults | | Faults | |
|---|---|---|---|
| Steering | ☐ | Exhaust | ☑ |
| Brakes | ☐ | Tyres | ☑ |
| Gears | ☐ | Wheels | ☐ |
| Mirror | ☐ | Bodywork | ☐ |
| Lights: headlights | ☑ | Other | ☐ |
| sidelights | ☐ | Insurance | ☐ |
| indicators | ☐ | Licence | ☑ |

## **Use of English:** Question forms

### Six Men in a Bath

A press conference was called last night after a one-legged man, two grandfathers and three fishermen escaped in a bathtub from a sinking trawler.

The men were on their way home to Whitehaven from the Isle of Man when the 40 ft boat went down. Reporters asked why the trawler had been carrying a bathtub, and were told that two of the men had made the outward journey from Whitehaven in the bathtub accompanied by the trawler to raise money for charity. When asked how the bathtub itself had floated, the men explained that it had been made specially watertight and buoyant for the charity trip.

The trawler, which had no life raft, was half way across the channel when it sank without warning, but the bathtub floated free and the men managed to climb in.

A reporter from Whitehaven wanted to know how long they had had to wait before being rescued, and was told that the helicopter had arrived after four hours.

Asked how they felt now they were safe, the men said they could not begin to describe their relief about being back on dry land. Before they left to return to their families, they were asked if they would ever put to sea again. The men replied that it would be a long time before they felt happy in a boat or a bath.

Complete the dialogue below between the reporters and the survivors.

Reporter: (1) Why ..........................................?

Survivor: (2) Two of us made the outward journey ..........................................

Reporter: (3) How ..........................................?

Survivor: (4) It had been made specially ..........

..........................................................

Reporter: (5) How long ....................................?

Survivor: (6) The helicopter ..............................

Reporter: (7) How ............................................?

Survivor: (8) We can't begin ..............................

Reporter: (9) ......................................................

Survivor: (10) ....................................................

## **Use of English:** Sentence transformation

Complete the sentences in such a way that they mean exactly the same as the sentence above.

**1** Susan asked what time the next train to London left.

'What ........................................................?'

**2** 'How long have you been here?' Peter asked the boy.

Peter asked the boy how ..............................

..........................................................................

**3** 'Are you staying in England for longer than a month?' the customs officer asked the tourists.

The customs officer asked the tourists ..........

..........................................................................

**4** 'Will you come and see me again?' the old man asked his granddaughter.

The old man asked his granddaughter

..........................................................................

## **Communication Activity:** Can we build a better future?

You are going to discuss this topic. Your teacher will put you into groups. First, read your roles overleaf and then give your opinions on the texts.

Chairpeople

> What problems will the world be facing in the future?
>
> You have called experts to a meeting in the hope of finding some solutions.
>
> You have also invited representatives from the world of politics, farming, industry, the developing countries, and the ordinary family.
>
> Open the meeting and welcome the speakers.
>
> During the meeting, make sure that everyone has a chance to speak, and keep notes so that you can sum up the main points when you end the meeting.

The Environmentalists

> What problems will the world be facing in the future?
>
> How do you think we can build a better future?

The Technologists

> What problems will the world be facing in the future?
>
> How do you think we can build a better future?

Representatives of the developing countries.

> Discuss the problems you are facing now, and how you see the future.

Listen to the experts and give your reactions to their solutions in groups.

**A**

There seems to be no end to the problems facing the world today and the implications for the future are terrifying. Will we have run out of fossil fuels and be living in a world without the comforts we have all become used to? Will we have blown ourselves up in a senseless war and will the survivors be living in a world more primitive than our ancestors'? Or will we have found the solutions necessary to overcome these immense problems? . . .

**B**

Think what we are doing to our world. We buy a car, which we replace in ten years or less. The car is made of metals which are rapidly running out. It is powered by petrol which fills the air with poison and noise. This is just one example of the thoughtless way industrial countries are treating the only home we have to live in. We must stop thinking of the world as a source of infinite materials, and a dustbin for all our toxic waste. We must change our way of life. There is no other solution. We cannot keep using chemicals to grow our food, or we'll pollute the rivers and seas irreversibly. We must stop experimenting with dangerous technology or an unthinkable catastrophe will destroy large parts of the world. Technological progress is not the only way forward . . .

**C**

A future where scientists will be treated like pop stars, where people shop and work in underground cities, where submarines will be carrying freight under the North Pole from China and where many of the world's diseases will have been eradicated. This is the vision of the experts who were painting their picture of the future for industrialists at a conference in London on Tuesday. Scientists criticised the so-called Green dream. 'They say we will be abandoning many consumer goods, but say nothing of the millions of workers who produce them. They say we'll be eating food produced without the help of chemical fertilizers, but say nothing of the higher prices we'll have to pay.' The experts at the conference agreed that with enough financial support for research, breakthroughs in science and technology will provide the answers to all today's problems.

**D**

There has been much talk in the papers about the debate over which direction the developed countries should take in the future. Yet little is said about the millions who live in the developing nations. We need 'development'; we need improved living standards. Do we believe the technologists who want to help us with huge expensive projects and more scientific methods? These cost us money and make us rely on the west to buy our products and crops. The Greens want us to develop our traditional approaches, but how does that help us to improve the quality of life of our people? We don't want to be debtors providing the industrialised world with a cheap source of raw materials, but we also don't want to be left as backward and underdeveloped. What we need is to be self-reliant and able to take decisions for ourselves.

### Useful Language

Language of discussion (formal)

I agree entirely.
You're quite right.
Exactly.
That's just what I think.

Could I say something here?
If I may interrupt . . .
Could I make a point here?

I'm afraid I don't agree.
I'm sorry, but I think . . .
That's a good point, but . . .
Yes, but . . .

## **Vocabulary:** Word building

### 1 -or / -er

These suffixes are used to make nouns from verbs.

**A** What is the difference in meaning between:

an invention an inventor an exploration an explorer

**B** Complete the following sentences using a suitable form of the word in CAPITALS:

**1** The .......... asked the candidates several difficult questions at the end of the test. (EXAMINE)

**2** The Soviets are here as .......... and will not speak at the conference. (OBSERVE)

**3** Richard Branson is well-known as a .......... of new rock bands. (PROMOTE)

**4** I have always been a great .......... of your work. (ADMIRE)

**5** Nowadays it is not always the man who is the .......... for the family. (PROVIDE)

**6** The letter was addressed to the .......... of the house. (OCCUPY)

**7** Since she's got that new job she's been acting like a .......... (DICTATE)

**8** Until his death he was well known as a .......... of modern art. (COLLECT)

**9** With your talent for languages you could get a job as a .......... (TRANSLATE)

**10** He started as a .......... of foreign cars. (DISTRIBUTE)

## 2 -en

This suffix is used to make verbs from nouns.

lengthen widen strengthen broaden
deepen weaken deafen darken
moisten heighten

Use ONE of the verbs above to complete each of the following sentences:

**1** The families were .......... by their lack of food and gradually all fell ill.

**2** Her skirt was too short so she had to .......... it.

**3** To .......... the roads the Council demolished the buildings on either side of the street.

**4** When the group started playing they were so loud that I thought it would .......... me.

**5** After the earthquake the government spent millions of pounds to .......... the remaining buildings.

**6** The sky began to .......... and we realised it was going to rain.

**7** As we flew over the countryside we saw the Nile River .......... as it flowed to the sea.

**8** Her eyes .......... as she began to cry.

**9** Living in the Sudan .......... his understanding of the problems of hunger and homelessness.

**10** The delay .......... the expectations of the crowd.

## **Writing:** Composition: Leaving instructions

You are going away on a long business trip and have decided to rent out your apartment. You must leave a letter explaining how to use the facilities.

Remember to be clear. Try to imagine how to do the things you want to explain. For example:

This is just a short note to explain how to use some of the machines in the flat.
If you want a bath then the water needs turning on half an hour before. The diagram next to the boiler will show you how to switch it on. Remember to light the pilot light before switching on the timer. You can video a TV programme without watching the TV .................
.......................................................................
.......................................................................
I hope you will enjoy your stay here. If you have any problems, please contact the agent.

### Useful Language

you need to + inf.
it needs to be + past participle
it needs + ing
to tell someone how to
show
explain x

**Compositions (between 120 and 180 words):**

**1** You are going away for the weekend and have asked a friend to look after your house while you are not there. Leave instructions telling your friend how to feed your pet cat and goldfish and what to do about the heating.

**2** Some important visitors are coming to your home. You have employed a cleaner to get the house ready for the guests. Write what you would say to him or her before you leave for work.

UNIT 13

# Money and the Criminal World

## Reading: The perfect crime

Read the first paragraph and cover the rest of the text. Try to answer the questions before going on to read the next paragraph.

Many thieves have found it difficult to resist the temptation of going on a spending spree when they find a credit card in a stolen wallet. Most of these criminals, however, are caught, arrested, charged with fraud and either given a heavy fine or sent to prison. Not always, though. There is one man whose identity is still unknown and who has managed to get away with probably the biggest ever credit card fraud. Estimates vary, but the police guess the man escaped with as much as £9 million of stolen goods, services and cash.

**STOP**

**1** How do you think he could have done it?

This may in fact be an example of the perfect crime. It was only discovered by accident when a bank clerk noticed the similarity between the handwriting on two different applications for a credit card. This was all the more strange because both forms had been sent from the same address. Someone was applying for cards using different names.

**STOP**

**2** How could he have stolen so much money?

To get a credit card an applicant must give details of his salary and bank account numbers and references. The details on the two forms were checked and were found to be correct. Even the signatures were good. Detectives working on the case found that these two were not the only cards illegally obtained. Thousands had been sent to the same address. When the police raided the house they found the floor literally carpeted with credit cards.

**STOP**

**3** How might the man have got details for thousands of cards?

The police also discovered that the man had placed a newspaper advertisement giving details of a highly paid, but obviously non-existent, job overseas. In the application form he sent to the 4,000 people who replied, he asked for the same information that a credit card company would need.

**STOP**

**4** How could he have spent such a large sum of money without getting caught?

He then used the details of the people to apply for thousands of credit cards from many different companies. When he got the cards he used the maximum limit allowed in one day on each card on the day it arrived. He only used each card once and spread his purchases around. To avoid detection he organised all of this in a very busy two weeks.

**STOP**

**5** Why didn't the police find him?

The thief transferred the money from bank to bank to building society to make it difficult for anyone to trace him. He then transferred all the money abroad and left the country himself. He didn't even pay for the newspaper advertisement and to this day he hasn't been caught.

## **Use of English:** Sentence transformation

Change these sentences to mean the same as those printed above.

**1** It's possible he was innocent.

He ...................................................................

**2** I'm certain he didn't take the money – he was out of the country at the time.

He ...................................................................

**3** It's possible he was a foreigner.

He ...................................................................

**4** I'm sure I left the heating on because the house is very warm.

I must ...................................................................

**5** I'm positive you didn't see him in town yesterday – he's still on holiday.

You ...................................................................

## **Vocabulary:** Prepositions

Which prepositions go with these verbs in the following story?

**1** Fred Smith broke .......... a house through a bedroom window.

**a** out **b** into **c** across **d** down

**2** Unfortunately the alarm went .......... and woke the neighbours.

**a** out **b** in **c** through **d** off

**3** The police arrived and arrested him .......... breaking and entering.

**a** for **b** to **c** by **d** without

**4** They also suspected him .......... other petty offences in the area.

**a** to **b** for **c** of **d** in

**5** They accused him .......... stealing the Mayor's car.

**a** of **b** down **c** for **d** to

**6** At the police station he was charged .......... five other offences.

**a** of **b** in **c** by **d** with

**7** In court, the jury found him guilty and the judge sentenced him .......... five years in jail.

**a** off **b** with **c** to **d** on

**8** He tried to break .......... seven times but was always caught before he got away.

**a** over **b** out **c** through **d** down

**9** Now Fred Smith has given .......... the life of crime.

**a** to **b** away **c** in **d** up

**10** He has taken .......... escapology as a means of earning a living instead.

**a** to **b** away **c** out **d** over

## **Communication Activity:** Interview practice

Discuss this picture with a partner.

### Advice on Discursive Composition (Paper 2)

Here you can be completely one-sided if you like.

You are asked for your own opinion and although you can refer to others, you may give only your own ideas.

It is also necessary to give reasons for your opinions and a good idea to make suggestions of what to do as well.

The opening paragraph and closing paragraphs should deal with the subject in general, giving the examiner an idea of what you are going to talk about and what decisions you have come to.

## **Writing:** Discursive composition

### Giving opinions and making suggestions

Example title:

Do you think prison sentences are too long?

**Planning Notes**

*Paragraph 1*
General Introduction

Why send people to prison?
Punishment? Revenge? Rehabilitation?
General safety of the public?

*Paragraph 2*
Personal Opinion & Reasons

Violent criminals need punishment and the public needs to be protected.

Lesser crimes need payment to victim – outside prison.

*Paragraph 3*
Suggestions

Longer prison sentences for violent/serious crimes; community work for minor offences.

*Paragraph 4*
Conclusion

Work with another student and make planning notes for one of the following compositions:

**1** The most important person is the victim, not the criminal. How should criminals be made to compensate their victims?

**2** Many city streets are becoming dangerous. What do you think should be done?

**3** Do you think that the police should be armed?

### Useful Language

In my opinion

| | | |
|---|---|---|
| I | | |
| Few people | think | |
| Some people | believe | that |
| A few people | would agree | |
| Many people | feel | |
| Most people | | |

It would be a good idea to
better

| | |
|---|---|
| We | |
| Society | should |
| They | |

To sum up
In other words

## **Listening:** Heroic failures

Listen to the passages and tick these statements: True or False.

| | TRUE | FALSE |
|---|---|---|
| **1** The first gang were unfamiliar with Vancouver. | | |
| **2** They didn't realise it was the same petrol station. | | |
| **3** The attendant had been tied up securely. | | |
| **4** They had a reliable car. | | |
| **5** The second criminal was on holiday. | | |
| **6** He stole only dirty things. | | |
| **7** He had a bath because he was tired. | | |
| **8** The third criminal was too heavy for the boat. | | |
| **9** He couldn't swim. | | |

## **Use of English:** Sentence transformation

Rewrite these sentences to mean the same as all those above.

**1** Leaving the safe unlocked was stupid.

The owners ...................................................

**2** It's a great shame I met those criminals.

I wish ...........................................................

**3** It wasn't a good idea for us to rob the bank in daylight.

We should ....................................................

**4** It's a pity I left my keys inside.

If only ..........................................................

**5** I'm sorry I didn't listen to the police.

I wish ...........................................................

## **Reading:** A morning at the CAB

The Citizens Advice Bureau is run mainly by volunteers who give up part of their week to help people who don't know who to turn to. They deal with ordinary people, with ordinary or extraordinary problems, some legal, some personal, some financial, some concerned with consumer goods, others with government grants and benefits.

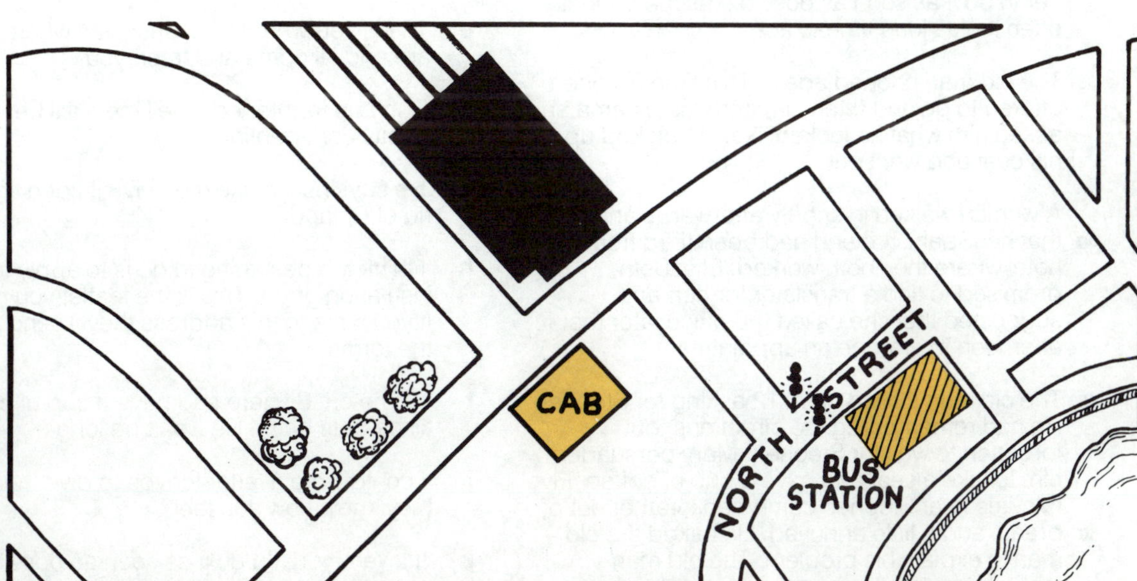

Mary, Stephen and Elisabeth were on duty on the day we visited the office. At 10 o'clock, when the doors opened, a young man with shadows under his eyes came in with a story about his noisy neighbours. Mary listened attentively and then suggested writing a formal letter of complaint for him. She invited him into the inner office to compose it.

The telephone rang and Stephen gave directions to the office to an old man phoning from the bus station. In the meantime, a young girl had come into the office and was looking at the leaflets on display on the coffee table. Elisabeth encouraged her to talk, and she said she was worried about her landlord. He had threatened to evict her because she had a pet rat. Elisabeth asked her to bring in a copy of her lease and the girl promised to bring it in later.

The phone rang again. The old man had forgotten the directions and was now outside the cinema. Stephen patiently explained how to find the office again.

Mary and the young man came out of the inner office with the letter. She reminded him to post it and he left still looking tired, but more relaxed.

A few minutes later a pensioner entered. It was autumn and getting colder, and she was very anxious about her winter heating bills. Mary recommended that she should apply for a grant to insulate her house and showed her a leaflet that explained how to go about it. She advised her to do it as soon as possible as the council often took a long time to act.

The old man phoned again. This time Stephen offered to go and fetch him from the cinema and asked him what he looked like. He picked up his coat and went out.

A woman walked in shortly afterwards and said that her Spanish friend had been fired from the hotel where they both worked. Elisabeth promised to find a translator for her, and suggested that she called the office later that afternoon to arrange an appointment.

The old man turned up at 12 asking for Stephen. He had remembered the directions, but forgotten to wait for Stephen. Mary persuaded him to take a seat and have a cup of coffee. Five minutes later Stephen came back, rather out of breath and a little annoyed. He asked the old man to explain his problem. The old man looked puzzled. He hadn't got a problem, he just wanted a chat with someone, and he had heard they made good coffee here. Stephen laughed and suggested they should all go to the cafe across the road for a sandwich and invited the old man to join them.

Exercise

Find the sentences in the passage which match those below. The first one has been done for you:

Example

'If you're at the bus station, you walk away from the sea, turn left into North Street, and turn right at the traffic lights. Keep going up the hill and we're opposite the station on the left.'

Answer

Stephen gave directions to the office.

**a** 'I'll definitely bring it in later,'

**b** 'Would you like to come with us?'

**c** 'Don't forget to get it in the post today,'

**d** 'Let's all go and have a bite to eat across the road?'

**e** 'I'll tell you what I'll do. Just stay where you are and I'll come and fetch you.'

**f** 'Don't be frightened to tell me – it'll be strictly confidential,'

**g** 'He says he'll make me leave if I don't get rid of Roland,'

**h** 'I think the best thing to do is to apply for an insulation grant. This is the leaflet you need. If you write to this address they'll send you the forms,'

**i** 'Come on. Sit here and have a cup of coffee till he gets back. He won't be long,'

**j** 'I could write a letter for you to give them so they know how you feel?'

**k** 'If I were you, I'd do it as soon as possible, as they tend to take their time,'

## **Communication Activity:** Role play

Students A: You are *Counsellors* working at the Citizens Advice Bureau.

Look at the information on your role card.

Be prepared to give advice where you can.

Remember to be sympathetic.

### Useful Language:

| Expressing sympathy: | Encouragement: |
|---|---|
| I'm so sorry. | Go on. |
| I'm sorry to hear that. | mmm. |
| That is a pity. | I quite understand. |
| That's terrible. | I see what you mean. |

Students A

*Notes for Counsellors*

Remember: you do not have to solve every problem yourself.

Here are some contact numbers/ addresses you can use to refer clients to the experts:

Problems with benefits/ grants for emergency repairs: D.H.S.S. Tel.: 702334

Legal problems: free advice – debts, the police, immigration, visas: Rights Centre 14 Trafalgar St. Open: 10 a.m.– 12.30 p.m. Mon–Fri

Problems with neighbours: Environmental Health Department Tel: 890990 (See also Letter of Complaint file)

Students B

You are clients. You have a problem and have decided to go to the CAB for advice. Decide what your problem is, what you want to do, what help you need.

# *Mock Examination*

## PAPER 1 READING COMPREHENSION (1 HOUR)

### SECTION A

*In this section you must choose the word or phrase which best completes each sentence. Give one answer only to each question.*

1 The stewardess took his ticket and put the suitcase on the machine to . . . . . . . . . . . . . . . its weight.
A test B examine C control D check

2 '. . . . . . . . . . . . . . . going to the zoo next Sunday?'
A How about B Let's C Why don't we D Shall we

3 I just . . . . . . . . . . . . . . . on my way home to see how you were.
A called off B called in C called away D called for

4 My car's broken down again. I wonder if you could . . . . . . . . . . . . . . . me yours?
A borrow B rent C lend D hire

5 I won't . . . . . . . . . . . . . . . you to come if you don't want to.
A make B let C force D allow

6 I'll tell you his name in a minute, it's on the . . . . . . . . . . . . . . . of my tongue.
A top B end C tip D point

7 The people were so . . . . . . . . . . . . . . . , they always said hello and even invited us for meals.
A sympathetic B friendly C sensitive D sensible

8 There was a tennis . . . . . . . . . . . . . . . at the back of the house.
A court B pitch C ground D stadium

9 I was . . . . . . . . . . . . . . . from attending the meeting by the train strike.
A avoided B protected C prevented D defended

10 . . . . . . . . . . . . . . . owning three houses in Europe, he also has an apartment in New York.
A Not only B Even C In addition D As well as

11 Don't drink the tap water . . . . . . . . . . . . . . . it's not clean.
A unless B otherwise C or else D in case

12 Your hair's getting too long, it . . . . . . . . . . . . . . . cutting.
A needs B should C ought to D merits

13 Take this . . . . . . . . . . . . . . . to the chemist who will give you the medicine you need.
A order B prescription C bill D receipt

14 The sun . . . . . . . . . . . . . . . over the horizon.
A lifted B raised C got up D rose

15 She . . . . . . . . . . . . . . . me the way to the station.
A said B told C explained D directed.

16 I'm well qualified for the post, and I've got a lot of . . . . . . . . . . . . . . . in the field.
A experiences B experience C experiments D knowledge

17 He . . . . . . . . . . . . . . . on seeing the manager.
A demanded B wanted C wished D insisted

18 Alexandria is situated on the coast at the . . . . . . . . . . . . . . . of the River Nile.
A head B source C foot D mouth

19 They set . . . . . . . . . . . . . . . on their holiday with a car laden with bulging suitcases and excited children.
A up B out C in D back

20 In his new job he . . . . . . . . . . . . . . . over £25,000.
A earns B wins C gains D obtains

21 Our . . . . . . . . . . . . . . . is being damaged by unscrupulous industrialists.
A climate B surroundings C wildlife D environment

22 We . . . . . . . . . . . . . . . booked. Look, the restaurant is empty.
A must have B can't have C needn't have D should have

23 He's only got . . . . . . . . . . . . . . . injuries, so he doesn't have to go to hospital.
A serious B grave C little D minor

24 The box . . . . . . . . . . . . . . . a hammer, an electric drill and a handful of nails and screws.
A contained B consisted of C composed of D comprised

25 The Lord Mayor's Show is one of the year's most colourful . . . . . . . . . . . . . . .
A possibilities B occasions C chances D opportunities

## SECTION B

### FIRST PASSAGE

Behind the Mason Arms, the pub which stood next door to the cottage my father had taken for the summer, and of which it formed a part, there was a yard surrounded by various dilapidated sheds and a piece of ground overgrown with grass and weeds which contained various interesting pieces of ancient rusted machinery, the most important of which was an old motor-car smelling of decaying rubber and dirty engine oil. I played with my best friend in the village, Peter Hutchings, whose mother kept a grocery, sweet and hardware store on the corner opposite the butcher's. It was from Peter Hutchings that I learned the broad local dialect which was so strong that by the end of the first summer at Branscombe no-one except a local inhabitant could understand what I was saying.

There in the inn yard in the long summer evenings we used to sit in the old motor car, either Peter or myself at the wheel, taking it in turn, the driver making BRRRing noises, the one sitting next to him in the front seat making honking noises – the horn had long ceased to be – as we roared around imaginary corners, narrowly missing imaginary vehicles coming in the opposite direction, driving through an imaginary world to an imaginary destination on an imaginary road, a pair of armchair travellers. In the back we used to put Betty Hutchings, if she was available, who wore a white beret, was placid, said nothing, apart from an occasional BRRR, and was in fact an ideal backseat passenger.

When we got tired of driving our car we ourselves used to become motor cars, tearing up and down the street outside making BRRRing noises of varying intensity as we changed gear, disturbing the elderly ladies who used to sit at their cottage doors making lace, the principal manufacture of the village. Close by, over the hill at Beer, where there were stone quarries, the quarrymen's wives had made the lace for Queen Victoria's wedding dress in 1839, an event that was still talked about in the neighbourhood more or less as if it had happened yesterday.

26 The writer's father had rented
- A a cottage with a yard.
- B a cottage behind a pub.
- C a cottage beside a pub.
- D a building containing a pub.

27 Who was Peter Hutchings?
- A A teacher.
- B The son of a local shopkeeper.
- C The only person who spoke the local dialect.
- D The author's only friend in the village.

28 When playing in the car
- A the writer always steered.
- B the two boys took it in turns to use the horn.
- C Betty never sat in the driver's seat.
- D they used to drive it around the village.

29 In the boys' opinion the perfect backseat passenger
- A said very little.
- B made noises like an engine.
- C was a girl.
- D wore a hat.

30 The old motor car
- A was part of the boys' fantasy games.
- B contained two armchairs.
- C was very noisy.
- D disturbed old ladies.

31 We understand from the story that
- A local women made Queen Victoria's wedding dress.
- B Queen Victoria's wedding was a very important occasion for the villagers.
- C it was written over 100 years ago.
- D the village's main industry was stone quarrying.

SECOND PASSAGE

For ten years John Grimshaw has been pioneering a gentle revolution. He aims to get us going by bike on Britain's network of disused railways. He works for Sustrans, a Bristol-based charity, as an engineer and he reckons highway engineers have got it wrong.

He believes that there is no benefit or logic behind the building of bigger and faster roads that only encourage people to use cars more extravagantly. Britain's roads are being built with disregard for all but the motorist while miles of railway tracks no longer used by trains lie wasted.

His organisation started work in 1979 with a modest five-mile track from Bristol to Bath and cyclists and walkers now make a million journeys a year on the path. Sustrans has since completed a further 150 miles throughout Britain with the help of volunteer workers.

Building such paths is not easy or cheap. Sustrans buys or leases land from British Rail and the paths can cost from £3,000 up to £40,000 per kilometre to build. Money comes from central and local government, charity bodies and gifts from individuals.

To encourage the more reluctant walkers and cyclists along its paths Sustrans plans to construct a work of art on every mile of path it builds. Most of their tracks quickly transport people from the city to the countryside. The latest route runs from the heart of Glasgow to Loch Lomond. Relics of the great railway age litter the routes – station houses, platforms, signal boxes and even steam trains.

Some might consider John Grimshaw a traveller from the past, out of touch with the modern world, but for many he is preparing the way for an alternative for a car-mad world.

32 The aim of Sustrans is
- A to encourage people to use cars more efficiently.
- B to use old railway lines for leisure purposes.
- C to provide a cycling network across Britain.
- D to build better and faster roads.

33 The Bath-to-Bristol line
- A is now 150 miles long.
- B has been open for over 10 years.
- C is used by a million cyclists a year.
- D was built by volunteers.

34 How does Sustrans finance its work?
- A With money from British Rail.
- B With a mixture of grants and donations.
- C By leasing its land.
- D By using volunteer workers.

35 The tracks
- A are not very popular.
- B use railway equipment as works of art.
- C are very short.
- D have been built in many parts of the country.

36 Sustrans
- A will not build any more tracks after Glasgow to Loch Lomond.
- B will have to clear the track of rubbish.
- C makes the countryside more accessible to the public.
- D believes more people will use their tracks in future.

THIRD PASSAGE

It makes sense to plan ahead.

As a Co-op VISA card holder you know it makes sense to budget and plan ahead. Because whatever you do and whatever your hobbies are – accidents can happen.

And if your Co-op Visa card repayments are unprotected, accident, sickness or unemployment can be a real headache for you and your family. The last thing you want to think about if you're unwell is money, after all.

Security and peace of mind.

That's why we've introduced the Co-op Care Plan. It's a common-sense way of protecting you and your family against a day when you might not be able to meet your repayments.

Whether you can't move because of an accident, sickness or unemployment – Co-op Visa Care Plan protects your repayments. The cost of the minimum repayments on your Visa card at the time of your misfortune will be paid each month.

And it costs you so little too!

All you pay to be included in the Co-op Visa Care Plan is 45p for each £100 of outstanding debit balance – at each statement date per month. It's as simple as that. You'll find full details on the reverse of this leaflet that show you how much sense it makes.

To join the Care Plan you must be under 61 years of age and in good health. Just complete your name and address and account number on the attached form, sign it and return it to us in the enclosed Freepost envelope – you won't even need a stamp. And then you can relax in the knowledge that your repayments are protected whatever turns up.

37 The Care Plan is designed for
- A people with families.
- B some Visa Credit Card holders.
- C people with headaches.
- D unhealthy people.

38 The Care Plan works by
- A protecting your family.
- B paying you when you are unemployed.
- C guaranteeing some of your credit card bills.
- D lending you money to pay your monthly bills.

39 If you had £270 owing on your Visa card at the end of the month, the Care Plan would cost you

A £145.
B 45p.
C £1.35p.
D £1.45p.

40 Care Plan is available to

A anyone with no history of illness.
B all Visa Card account holders.
C people under 61 who are fit.
D only people with families.

## PAPER 2 COMPOSITION (1½ HOURS)

*Write two only of the following compositions. Your answers must follow exactly the instructions given and must be of between 120 and 180 words.*

1 You are thinking of spending a weekend seeing the sights in your capital city. Write a letter to some friends inviting them to join you and describing some of the things you are planning to do.

2 You recently took your employer out to a restaurant to impress him/her. Unfortunately the evening was a disaster. Tell the story of what happened.

3 'Win a new house! Tell us what your fantasy home would be.' Write what you would send in to enter this competition.
or
Describe your ideal house.

4 'These days people don't talk to each other enough.' Give your opinion of this statement.

# PAPER 3 USE OF ENGLISH (2 HOURS)

## SECTION A

1 *Fill in each of the numbered blanks with* **one** *suitable word.*

The Hotel X was (1) . . . . . . . . vast, impressive building with a classical facade, and at one side a little dark doorway (2) . . . . . . . . a rat-hole, which was the service entrance. I arrived (3) . . . . . . . . a quarter to seven (4) . . . . . . . . the morning. Groups of men (5) . . . . . . . . hurrying in and being checked (6) . . . . . . . . a doorkeeper (7) . . . . . . . . sat in a tiny office. I waited and (8) . . . . . . . . the assistant manager came (9) . . . . . . . . show me (10) . . . . . . . . I was going to work.

He led me down a winding (11) . . . . . . . . into a narrow passage, deep underground with a (12) . . . . . . . . which was (13) . . . . . . . . low that I (14) . . . . . . . . to bend my head in places. (15) . . . . . . . . was stiflingly hot and very dark. It (16) . . . . . . . . me of the lower (17) . . . . . . . . of a liner; there was the same heat and cramped space and unappetising (18) . . . . . . . . of food, and a humming, whirring noise which came (19) . . . . . . . . the kitchen furnaces but which (20) . . . . . . . . just like the whir of engines.

2 *Finish each of the sentences in such a way that it means exactly the same as the sentence printed before it.*

EXAMPLE:

It took me 5 hours to get there.

I spent ..........................................................................................

Answer: I spent 5 hours getting there.

a) Someone will serve you in a moment.

You ..........................................................................................

b) This is the most spectacular view I've ever seen.

I've ..........................................................................................

c) 'You'd better take an umbrella in case it rains', he told her.

He advised ..........................................................................................

d) The optician tests my eyes every six months.

I have ..........................................................................................

e) The last time I spoke French was ten years ago.

I have ..........................................................................................

f) The train was delayed so I arrived late.

If ..........................................................................................

g) The old car accelerates more quickly than the new one.

The new car ..........................................................................................................

h) It was foggy but they continued to drive fast.

They ..........................................................................................................

i) It's a pity she sings so badly.

If only ..........................................................................................................

j) They don't work as hard as they did before.

They used ..........................................................................................................

3 *Write in the space in each of the following sentences the correct phrase made from PUT.*

a) However irritating they are, we must . . . . . . . . . . . . . . . them because they're our relatives.

b) They . . . . . . . . . . . . . . . the match until the following Saturday because of the bad weather conditions.

c) Could you . . . . . . . . . . . . . . . the light, please, it's dark in here.

d) Hold the line, please, I'll . . . . . . . . . . . . . . . to Mr Smith's secretary.

e) I . . . . . . . . . . . . . . . the new job, but I expect they'll turn me down.

4 *The word in capitals at the end of each of the following sentences can be used to form a word that fits suitably in the blank space. Fill each blank in this way.*

EXAMPLE:

All . . . . . . . . . . . . . . . are gratefully received. (DONATE)

Answer: donations

a) He was one of the greatest . . . . . . . . . . . . . . . of all time. (PERFORM)

b) The assistant was so . . . . . . . . . . . . . . . , he didn't even look to see if they had my size. (HELP)

c) The two countries are . . . . . . . . . . . . . . . very similar. (CULTURE)

d) Part of her lack of success is due to her . . . . . . . . . . . . . . . to think up original ideas. (ABLE)

e) Please confirm your . . . . . . . . . . . . . . . 48 hours before departure. (RESERVE)

5 *Complete the sentences suitably.*

RECEPTIONIST: Good morning. Can I help you?

1) STUDENT: ............................................................................................ ?
RECEPTIONIST: Certainly. We have several types of courses at this school: full-time and part-time general English courses, and evening courses in business English.

2 STUDENT: ............................................................................................ ?
RECEPTIONIST: Well, the lessons run from 7.30 to 9.30 in the evening.

3) STUDENT: ............................................................................................ ?
RECEPTIONIST: They are quite small, usually only about 3 students in the class.

4) STUDENT: ............................................................................................ ?
RECEPTIONIST: Yes, all our students sit a test at the beginning of the course so that we can put them in the right class.

5) STUDENT: ............................................................................................ ?
RECEPTIONIST: We've got a computer room, several videos, a small library and a canteen for the students.

6) STUDENT: ............................................................................................ ?
RECEPTIONIST: It depends how long you want to stay. Here is the brochure with all the details about prices at the back.

7) STUDENT: ............................................................................................ ?
RECEPTIONIST: I'm sorry, but I'm afraid this month is fully booked. There are some places available on the next course, though.

8) STUDENT: ............................................................................................ ?
RECEPTIONIST: Monday, 23 August.

9) STUDENT: ............................................................................................ ?
RECEPTIONIST: Of course. Just fill in this form here. We would like a £50 deposit if possible.

10) STUDENT: ............................................................................................ ?
A: Of course, we accept most credit cards.

## SECTION B

*Susan Jackson is enquiring about volunteer/community work. Using the information from the booklet below, complete the conversation between Susan and agent in the office in approximately 120 words.*

A

Gormorgor Agricultural Development Organisation, Freetown, Sierre Leone, W. Africa.
Farmwork volunteers to help on village farms to produce rice, maize, pineapples and bananas.
Age: 18+ Duration: 12 months.
Experience: not necessary.
Expenses: half board/accommodation provided. Travel/insurance not provided. Volunteers expected to contribute to costs of food.
Total: approx. £1,500.
Notes: volunteers should be independent and adaptable. Willing to live in isolated area.

B

Urban Trust, Manchester MB4 2H1
Playground Supervisors and Assistants.
Age: 18+ Duration: minimum 3 months from September.
Experience: not necessary but previous experience of working with children an advantage.
Expenses: food/accommodation not provided. Travel expenses to Manchester paid.
Salary £35 during training, £80 per week for leaders.
Notes: Candidates must be capable and imaginative with a good sense of humour and infinite patience.

C

Genesis II Talamca Cloud Forest, Costa Rica, Central America.
Conservation workers to help with construction and maintenance of paths in mountainous area.
Age: 17+ Duration: 1 month upwards (May–Dec).
Experience: preferred but basic training given. Some knowledge of Spanish helpful.
Expenses: volunteers contribute £30 per week to cover accommodation/meals and should allow approx. £1,750 to cover travel/insurance.
Notes: work involves physical labour at high altitude (2,360 m) – candidates should be fit and healthy. All nationalities welcome.

SUSAN: I'm interested in working on one of your schemes. Could you give me some more details about them?

AGENT: Certainly. Most of our positions available at the moment ....................................................

..........................................................................................................................................

..........................................................................................................................................

..........................................................................................................................................

..........................................................................................................................................

..........................................................................................................................................

SUSAN: And what sort of people are they looking for?

AGENT: ..........................................................................................

..........................................................................................

..........................................................................................

..........................................................................................

..........................................................................................

..........................................................................................

..........................................................................................

## PAPER 4 LISTENING COMPREHENSION (ABOUT 30 MINUTES)

### SECTION 1

*For questions 1–5 fill in the spaces in the following messages:*

Martha Spade is an artist and cartoonist who is often away from home. She has an answering machine for any messages and her husband usually writes them out for her. Fill in the gaps in his messages.

---

Messages for Tuesday:

1 Artists Supplies called. Your new paints have arrived but they're going to cost (1). . . . . . They've also got a special offer on paper.

2 Frank Jeffries from Good Homes and Gardens called about a meeting in London next Friday at (2). . . . . . with the Editor. They want the cover to be in colour.

3 Janet is having problems with the unit on (3). . . . . . She wants to know about the (4). . . . . . She's coming round tonight.

4 Terry Black from Greensense called about some drawings for their next magazine. Can you call them? Their number is 01–236–(5). . . . . .

---

**SECTION 2**

*For questions 6–10 mark the statements below True or False. Read the advertisement first. You are interested in pleasure cruises in the area and have rung up a local company.*

## SEASIDE CRUISES

*The best way to see the South Coast*

Welcome aboard our luxury boats!

Whether you want to sail along the beautiful English coastline or visit the splendour of rural France there is a SEA CRUISE for you!

Tickets include the price of meals, guided commentaries and accommodation as appropriate.

| | | TRUE | FALSE |
|---|---|---|---|
| 6) | Both cruises to Beachy Head include meals. | | |
| 7) | Tickets for the Isle of Wight cruise cannot be bought on ship. | | |
| 8) | There will be an English, French and German guide on the round-trip cruise. | | |
| 9) | Three breakfasts are included in the price of the French trip. | | |
| 10) | Passengers require valid travel documents for the Sea Empress cruise. | | |

## SECTION 3

*For question 11 tick the items mentioned in the programme. An example has been done for you.*

11)

| | | | | |
|---|---|---|---|---|
| 1 | Buying second-hand bicycles. | | 6 | Wearing suitable clothing. |
| 2 | Regular maintenance of bicycles. | | 7 | Riding in bad conditions. |
| 3 | Teaching children proper manoeuvrability. | √ | 8 | Looking at cars. |
| 4 | Instructions on riding in traffic. | | 9 | Improving children's sight. |
| 5 | Cycling at weekends. | | 10 | Safety devices for bicycles. |

## SECTION 4

*For question 12 you should tick one of the pictures (A, B, C or D). For questions 13–15 choose the answer that best completes or answers the question.*

12) Which of these pictures shows the first house the couple talk about?

13) The second and third houses
- A have four bedrooms each.
- B are fitted with kitchens.
- C have adequate gardens.
- D are ready for immediate occupation.

14)
- A The woman wants a house with a large garden and a study.
- B The man wants a house built on one floor.
- C The woman doesn't want a house with too many bedrooms.
- D The man doesn't want a garden that needs a lot of work.

15)
- A The woman sounds enthusiastic.
- B The man sounds impatient.
- C The woman sounds pessimistic.
- D The man sounds satisfied.

# PAPER 5 INTERVIEW (ABOUT 15 MINUTES)

*You will be asked to take part in a conversation with your teacher and/or some other students. The conversation will be based on one particular subject or theme, e.g. sport, the arts or travel for example.*

*Each interview is different but most students are asked to look at a photograph and discuss what they can see as well as more general ideas.*

*Students may then be asked to look at a reading passage and/or take part in a communication activity. All these activities are to give you an opportunity to speak so don't worry if you do not have exactly the same activities as other students.*

## INTERVIEW EXERCISES

### PHOTOGRAPH

Talk about the photograph on the inside back cover.

### COMMUNICATION ACTIVITY

**BBC1**

1.0 News, weather. 1.30 Neighbours*. 1.50 Film: His Kind of Woman-Robert Mitchum. 3.45 Gardener's Direct Line. 4.10 Ewoks. 4.35 Mysterious Cities of Gold. 5.0 Newsround. 5.05 We Are the Champions Special. 5.35 Neighbours*.

**6.00** NEWS. Weather. 6.30 Newsroom South East.

**7.00** TOP OF THE POPS.

**7.30** EASTENDERS*. Pat Butcher was last seen telling Frank that all she wanted was a normal family life, after his ghastly daughter Janine was eventually found. There seems little hope of finding this in Albert Square.

**8.00** BLANKETY BLANK*. More prizes and more Les Dawson with celebrity guests.

**8.30** IN SICKNESS AND IN HEALTH*. Alf Garnett is back having modified his opinions very little in 23 years. But he has learned a few tricks about buying council houses. With all his family long since driven out, his monotonous tirades are now directed at local bureaucrats, pub bores, and an unfortunate neighbour he plans to marry for financial reasons.

**9.00** NEWS. Weather.

**BBC2**

1.20 Pinny's House. 1.25 Bric A Brac. 1.35 International Golf. 5.30 Film 89.

**6.00** CRACK UP (1946) Pat O'Brien, Claire Trevor. *Nicely tangled thriller with a touch of Hitch here and there and Herbert Marshall giving a coolly authoritative performance in a plot about an art scam-AW.*

**7.30** THE VICTORIAN KITCHEN GARDEN*. July, and Harry suggests shooting raspberries (with bullets) to get rid of caterpillars.

**8.00** WILDLIFE SHOWCASE*. The hysterical Australian laughter of the Kookaburra.

**8.30** OPEN SPACE. Namibia, and the politically sensitive question of importing uranium.

**9.00** POLICE SQUAD. From the makers of the spoof film Airplane a new series about the adventures of the deadpan accident-prone detective who has a way of stumbling on the right answers by fluke. Frank Drebin (Leslie Nielson) an American Inspector Clouseau, strongly suspects the bank cashier, a family man who carries on rubber stamping as he slumps to the floor; by the time he is finished there are many more corpses.

**THAMES**

1.0 ITN News, weather. 1.20 Thames News, weather. 1.30 Heirloom. 2.0 A Country Practice. 3.0 P.S.I. 3.25 Thames News, weather. 3.30 Sons and Daughters. 4.0 Dogtanian and the Three Muskehounds. 4.25 T-Bag Bounces Back. 4.50 Scooby Doo. 5.10 Home and Away.

**5.40** ITN NEWS. 5.55 Thames News, weather.

**6.30** EMMERDALE FARM.

**7.00** HIGHWAY TO HEAVEN. The Monster, part one (of two). Romance between a blind woman and a reclusive artist.

**8.00** THE BILL*. Burnside does his best to make a detective out of Carver with very little success.

**8.30** CODED HOSTILE*. The dramatised story of the Korean Airlines jumbo shot down six years ago, with Michael Murphy, Chris Sarandon and Michael Moriarty as Washington big-wigs and Ronald Reagan playing the President for real. Most experts agreed that it looked like a genuine blunder by the Russians but this did not match the Cold War rhetoric of the time, especially as it involved confessing there was a spy plane in the area. So "provocation" it was. At all times of crisis—with World War III possibly looming—the big debate is whether or not to wake the President.

**10.00** NEWS AT TEN. 10.30 Thames News, weather.

**CHANNEL 4**

1.0 Sesame Street. 2.0 Gallery. 2.30 Racing from York. 4.30 Countdown.

**5.00** A WINDOW IN LONDON Michael Redgrave, Paul Lukas. *Redgrave is the young crane driver who thinks he has witnessed a murder when in fact he is about to get involved with the wife of a jealous magician. 1939 melodrama.*

**6.30** XERXES. Final episode of Swedish schoolboys about to leave home.

**7.00** CHANNEL 4 NEWS. 7.50 Comment, Weather.

**8.00** OPINIONS. Below the belt. Diminutive actor David Rappaport argues that life is a joke when seen from a height of 3ft 11in. Relationships with women provide a good laugh.

**8.30** BRASS. Return of the Yorkshire comedy with Timothy West as the ruthless 1930s industrial empire builder. The first of 13 repeats leading to a new series in the new year.

**9.00** A ZED AND TWO NOUGHTS Brian Deacon, Eric Deacon. *One of Peter Greenaway's totally individualistic movies, part surrealistic comedy, part intellectual puzzle, set in and around a zoo, but with the emphasis on the many variations of duality that the writer-director conjures out of his characters and situations-AW.*

You and your friend(s) are discussing what to watch on TV tonight. You disagree with each other so try to persuade the other people to change their minds as you have been looking forward to your programme for a long time.

### READING PASSAGES

A Next year English schoolchildren will be able to take another language exam if they choose. However, it might come as a surprise to learn that the new language offered is Esperanto. Maybe even more surprising is the fact that there are over 10,000 in Britain who can speak Esperanto according to the Esperanto Asocio de Briujo.

B Sunday. Day off. Paper in bed. Wander round my garden, then do food shopping. Six old friends coming to eat so I start cooking. Watch TV with my son while the chicken is cooking. Lay table and wait for guests to arrive. Finally all turn up. We have great time talking about the old days.

C Business is booming at tourist attractions, according to research into 3,327 places of interest by the English Tourist Board.

A survey of last year's visits published today shows wildlife and safari parks and zoos enjoyed the biggest jump in popularity.

Substantial investment and better marketing transformed falling attendances at wildlife attractions into a 28% increase over the years between 1982 and 1987.

# *Introduction to Spotlight on Language*

These units work in parallel with the main units in this book, except for the Introductory unit which has no specific grammatical basis. In other words the grammar points found in Spotlight on Language Unit 1, for example, will be among those covered in Unit 1 of the book.

The Spotlight on Language units exist for two main reasons – to act as a quick reference system when a grammar point needs revising and to give you extra self-study material that you can do in your own time. Each Spotlight on Language unit contains one or more exercises, to which the answers are at the end of the unit.

These units will also be useful for revision purposes as you get nearer the exam, and enable you to brush up on any weak points.

UNIT 1

# Spotlight on Language

## PRESENT SIMPLE ACTIVE

### FORM

| | | | | |
|---|---|---|---|---|
| Affirmative | Pronoun/noun + infinitive | | | |
| | I | sing. | | |
| Negative | Pronoun/noun + primary auxiliary (do) + not + infinitive | | | |
| | I | do | not | sing. |
| Interrogative | Primary auxiliary + pronoun/noun + infinitive | | | |
| | Do | you | sing? | |
| Negative interrogative | Primary auxiliary + pronoun/noun + not + infinitive | | | |
| | Do | you | not | sing? |
| Contraction | Don't | you | | sing? |

**NB** In speech and informal letters it is more common and correct to contract **do not** to **don't**.

In formal letters eg business letters it is better to use the full form.

The present simple forms of the verbs **have**, **do**, and **be** are as follows:

| | **have** | **do** | **be** |
|---|---|---|---|
| I | have | do | am |
| You | have | do | are |
| He/she/it | has | does | is |
| You | have | do | are |
| We | have | do | are |
| They | have | do | are |

For the third person singular in the affirmative add an **-s** to the infinitive. Exceptions to this rule are infinitives ending in:

a consonant + **y**: Change the **y** to **-ies**, eg **fry-fries**

a final **-o**; **-ch**; **sh**; **-ss**; **-x**: Add **-es** eg **go-goes**; **watch-watches**; **wash-washes**; **cross-crosses**; **box-boxes**.

# THE PRESENT SIMPLE PASSIVE

## FORM

| | Pronoun/noun + primary auxiliary (be) + past participle | | |
|---|---|---|---|
| Affirmative | Elephants | are | found in Africa. |

The forms of the negative, interrogative and negative interrogative are formed in the same way as for the active except that they use **be** instead of **do**.

### Exercise 1

For practice turn the following into negatives, interrogatives, and negative interrogatives.

**a** *That car is made of fibreglass.*
**b** *Those dresses are sold in Harrods.*
**c** *All salaries are increased annually.*

# THE PRESENT SIMPLE ACTIVE

## USES

The present simple is used to describe actions which:

**a** happen repeatedly, eg:

*I often go to the cinema.*

On the time line this looks like this:

**b** are habitual:

*I live in London.*

**c** happen at one particular time:

*I don't like this film.*

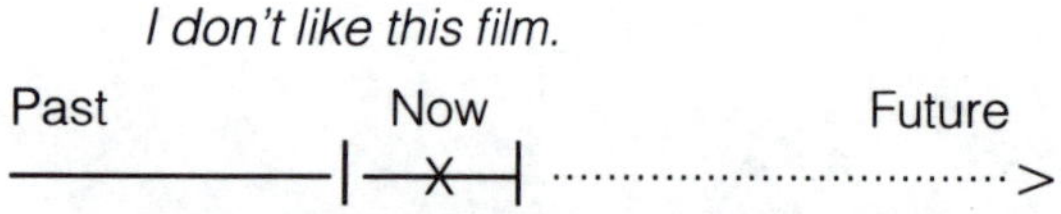


# THE PRESENT SIMPLE PASSIVE

## USES

The passive is easy to form in all the tenses. The only thing to decide is when it is better to use it than the active form. The following are the main uses and you can refer to them when you learn other tenses later on in the book.

**1** When we don't know the identity of the person who has done something we usually use the passive, eg:

*'This church was painted 300 years ago.'*

**2** When the identity of the person is less important than the action itself, eg:

*'Oil has been found in Alaska.'*

The passive is often used to describe how things are made, and this is specially true with scientific texts.

The passive is more often used to describe something in the past but there are times when we use the present simple passive. The most frequent occasions are:

**a** to speak or write about things which are habitual, eg:
*'A lot of French mustard is made in Dijon.'*

**b** to describe an official process:
*'A person who commits a crime is first arrested, then charged and taken to court where he is tried.'*

**c** to describe a scientific process:
*'The surface of the metal is first polished with diamond paste and then examined under a microscope.'*

# PRESENT PROGRESSIVE ACTIVE

## FORM

| | Pronoun/noun + primary auxiliary + present participle | | |
|---|---|---|---|
| Affirmative | It | is | raining. |

The forms of the negative, interrogative and negative interrogative follow the same pattern as the present simple except that the appropriate form of the auxiliary **be** is used instead of **do**.

**NB** In speech and informal letters it is more common and correct to contract:

| | |
|---|---|
| I am → I'm | I am not → I'm not |
| You are → you're | You are not → You aren't/You're not |
| He, She, It is → He's, She's, It's | He is not etc. → He isn't/He's not |
| We are → We're | We are not → We aren't/We're not |
| They are → They're | They are not → They aren't/They're not |

Similarly in the negative interrogative: **aren't I?**, **isn't it?** etc.

**Exercise 2**

For practice turn the following into negatives, interrogatives and negative interrogatives.

**a** It is raining.
**b** She is leaving now.
**c** They are playing football.

# PRESENT PROGRESSIVE PASSIVE

## FORM

| Personal pronoun/noun + primary auxiliary + past participle | | |
|---|---|---|
| The bedroom | is being | painted. |

**Exercise 3**

For practice turn the above sentence into the negative, interrogative and negative interrogative.

# PRESENT PROGRESSIVE ACTIVE

## USES

The present continuous is used to describe an action which is happening over a certain length of time but the length of time is seen by the speaker as being limited.

*It's raining*, looks like this on the time line:

# PRESENT PROGRESSIVE PASSIVE

## USES

This tense is used in the same ways as the active voice when the person/thing being done something to is more important than who or what is doing it, eg:

*George is repairing my car today.*

can be

*My car is being repaired today.*

when 'my car' is more important than 'George'.

# PRESENT SIMPLE and PRESENT PROGRESSIVE

The differences between the two tenses is easy to see on time lines. Look at these pairs of sentences and their time lines.

**a** *It rains a lot in England.*

**b** *It's raining.*

**a** *He hates being interviewed.*

**b** *He's being interviewed now.*

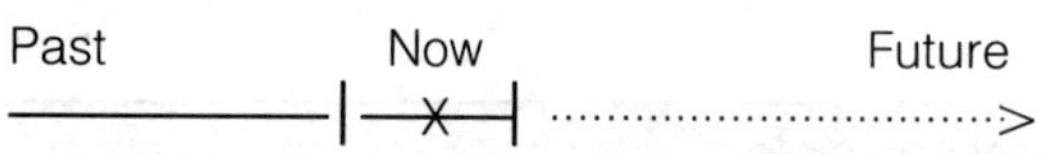


**Exercise 4**

Put the verbs in brackets into the correct tense. Use only the present simple or present progressive.

Victoria station (1. be) always busy. Many thousands of people (2. use) this station every day. Today it (3. rain) and most of the passengers (4. carry) umbrellas and (5. wear) raincoats. James (6. wait) for the arrival of a special friend. He frequently (7. look) at the information board for news about the boat train. It normally (8. arrive) on time but today he (9. know) the boats from France (10. have) trouble with the weather in the Channel. Suddenly there (11. be) an announcement – the train (12. be) delayed by half an hour.

# FREQUENCY ADVERBS

We use these adverbs to say how often something is done or how often we do something. Below are these adverbs in order from 100% (always) to 0% (never).

| | |
|---|---|
| 100% | always |
| 90% | generally, usually, regularly, normally |
| 80% | often, frequently |
| 40% | sometimes |
| 20% | occasionally |
| 10% | rarely, seldom |
| 0% | never. |

These adverbs usually go before the verb; eg:

*I often play tennis.*

But they always go after the verb **to be** when it is used as a main verb; eg:

*He is usually late.*

**Exercise 5**

In this exercise put the words in brackets into the sentence in the correct order.

**Example**: How *often do you play* tennis? (do play you often)

**1** I __________ to the cinema. (do go not usually)

**2** In Britain trains __________ late. (generally are)

**3** Tourists __________ into Buckingham Palace. (allowed are never)

**4** '__________ stay up late?' (you do often)

**5** 'No __________ in bed by 10 o'clock.' (normally am I)

# *Unit 1 Answers*

## EXERCISE 1

**a** That car is not made of fibreglass.
Is that car made of fibreglass?
Isn't that car made of fibreglass?

**b** Those dresses are not sold in Harrods.
Are those dresses sold in Harrods?
Aren't those dresses sold in Harrods?

**c** All salaries are not increased annually.
Are all salaries increased annually?
Aren't all salaries increased annually?

## EXERCISE 2

**a** It isn't raining.
Is it raining?
Isn't it raining?

**b** She isn't leaving now.
Is she leaving now?
Isn't she leaving now?

**c** They aren't playing football.
Are they playing football?
Aren't they playing football?

## EXERCISE 3

The bedroom isn't being painted.
Is the bedroom being painted?
Isn't the bedroom being painted?

## EXERCISE 4

**1** is
**2** use
**3** is raining
**4** are carrying
**5** wearing
**6** is waiting
**7** looks
**8** arrives
**9** knows
**10** are having
**11** is
**12** is

## EXERCISE 5

**1** I don't usually go to the cinema.
**2** In Britain trains are generally late.
**3** Tourists are never allowed into Buckingham Palace.
**4** 'Do you often stay up late?'
**5** No, I am normally in bed by 10 o'clock.

UNIT 2

# PAST SIMPLE ACTIVE

## FORM

| | | | | |
|---|---|---|---|---|
| Affirmative | Pronoun/noun + past tense | | | |
| | I | walked. | | |
| Negative | Pronoun/noun + primary auxiliary (did) + not + infinitive | | | |
| | I | did | not | walk. |
| Interrogative | Primary auxiliary + pronoun/noun + infinitive | | | |
| | Did | you | | walk? |
| Negative interrogative | Primary auxiliary + pronoun/noun + not + infinitive | | | |
| | Did | you | not | walk? |
| Contraction | Didn't | you | | walk? |

### Regular verbs

The past tense of regular verbs is formed by adding **-ed** to the infinitive, eg **walk-walked**, **play-played**, etc. When the infinitive has only one syllable and ends with a vowel followed by a consonant, the consonant is doubled, **shop-shopped**, **tap-tapped**, **chat-chatted**, **plan-planned**, etc.

When the infinitive has more than one syllable the final consonant is not usually doubled, eg **open-opened**, **alter-altered**, **disturb-disturbed**. It only doubles if it is part of the stressed syllable, **deter-detérred**, **infer-inférred**, etc.

For the past tense of the most common irregular verbs see the list on page (191).

The past tense of the verb **be** is **was** for the first and third person singular and **were** for all the other persons. The past tense for the verb **have** is **had** for all persons and for **do** is **did**.

# PAST SIMPLE PASSIVE

## FORM

| | | | | |
|---|---|---|---|---|
| Affirmative | Pronoun/noun + primary auxiliary + past participle | | | |
| | It | was | made | in Japan. |

The forms of the negative, interrogative and negative interrogative are formed in the same way as for the active except they use **was** and **were** instead of **did**.

### Exercise 1

For practice turn the following into negatives, interrogatives and negative interrogatives.

**a** *His car was stolen last week.*
**b** *The protesters were arrested.*
**c** *President Kennedy was assassinated by one person.*

# PAST SIMPLE ACTIVE

## USES

The past simple is used to describe actions which:

**a** happened repeatedly in the past, eg:

*I often hated school.*

On the time line this looks like this:

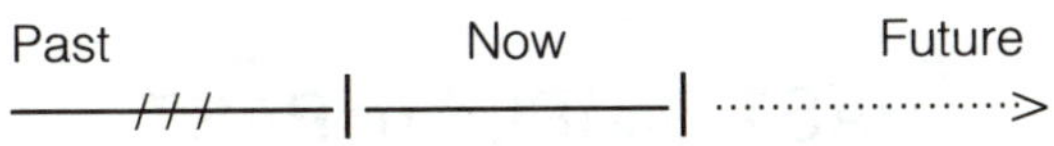


**b** happened over an extended period in the past, eg:

*I lived in Oxford for three years.*

On the time line this looks like this:

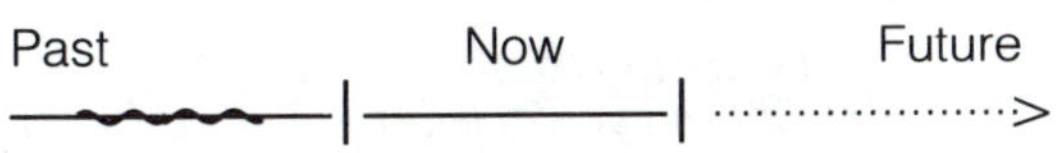


**c** happened at one particular time in the past.

*I met the Queen in 1968.*

On the time line this looks like this:

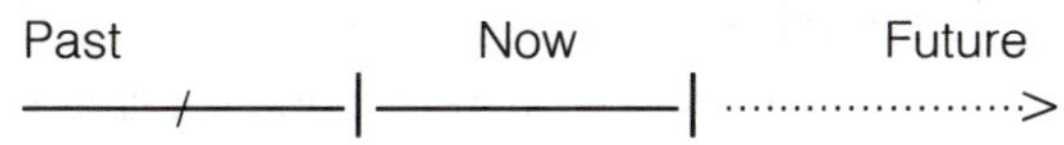


**d** happened as a sequence of events in the past.

*'The couple walked in, asked for a menu and ordered a meal. They ate their meal in silence, paid the bill and left the restaurant.'*

On the time line this looks like this:

# PAST SIMPLE PASSIVE

## USES

The uses of the passive are the same as those given on **Spotlight on Language p. 146**.

We use the passive far more in the past simple because we often speak or write about things that happened in the past and we can decide whether the person or thing that did something is or isn't more important than the person or thing it was done to. We usually think that we are fairly important so often we make ourselves the subject of the sentence, eg *I was hit by a car today*, rather than *A car hit me today.*

# PAST PROGRESSIVE ACTIVE

## FORM

| | Pronoun/noun + primary auxiliary + present participle | | |
|---|---|---|---|
| Affirmative | It | was | raining. |

The form of the negative, interrogative and negative interrogative follows the same pattern as the present progressive, see p. 147, except the auxiliaries used are the appropriate past tenses of **be**.

# PAST PROGRESSIVE PASSIVE

## FORM

| | Pronoun/noun + primary auxiliary + past participle | | |
|---|---|---|---|
| Affirmative | Coffee | was being | served. |

**Exercise 2**

For practice turn this sentence into the negative, interrogative and negative interrogative.

# PAST PROGRESSIVE ACTIVE

## USES

The past progressive is used to describe an action or sequence of actions which happened in the past over a certain length of time but the length of time was limited. The past progressive is used rather like the present progressive to talk or write about the background to a sequence of events. If we look again at the sequence of events described for use **d** of the past simple and then add some background it helps us see the different uses of the two tenses.

*It was raining heavily and people were returning home from work. The couple walked in, asked for a menu and ordered a meal. Around them the other diners were talking about the robbery or reading the newspaper stories about it. They ate their meal, paid the bill and left the restaurant. It was still raining.*

The past simple tells us the main events in the story, the past progressive gives us the background.

# PAST PROGRESSIVE PASSIVE

## USES

We use the past progressive passive when we want to speak or write about something that happened to someone or something over a limited period of time in the past.

*I walked to work because my car was being repaired.*

# PAST SIMPLE or PAST PROGRESSIVE

Sometimes when we see sentences like:

*I lived in Oxford* and *I was living in Oxford.*

It is difficult to see the difference between the two tenses. Now look at the two sentences in the context of a conversation.

A: *I went to Oxford yesterday.*
B: *Oh! did you? I lived in Oxford for ten years. It's a beautiful city isn't it?*

X: *How did you meet your wife?*
Y: *She was at university and I was living in Oxford at the time.*

The past simple is used to describe the main event and the past progressive gives the background.

**Exercise 3**

Read the following passage and put the verbs in brackets into the correct tense. Use only the past simple or the past progressive.

*Paul (1. get) up late as usual, (2. go) to the window and (3. look) out. For a change the sun (4. shine) and he (5. see) that the car park (6. be) already empty. He (7. have) a shower, (8. dress) and (9. drink) a quick cup of coffee. He (10. leave) the flat and (11. run) to the bus stop. A lot of people (12. wait) there, some (13. talk) but most (14. stand) in silence. The bus (15. arrive) and he (16. get) on. There (17. be) a lot of traffic on the road. The reason (18. be) soon clear, the road (19. repair). Paul (20. look) at his watch anxiously and (21. hope) that his boss (22. be) also late. He (23. arrive) at work half an hour late. He (24. notice) that everybody (25. work). A colleague (26. come) up to him and (27. say) 'The boss (28. look) for you. He wants to see you in his office.'*

# INTRODUCTORY SUBJECT

### There is/There are

We often use **There is** or **There are** before the subject of a sentence, eg:

*There isn't any milk in the fridge.*
*There's someone to see you.*
*There are two policemen at the door.*
*There's a stain on the carpet.*

We often use **There is/There are** to describe something we know or can see to somebody who does not know it or can't see it, for example, to describe a picture or photograph to someone.

*There's an old man in the picture. On the table in front of him there are a lot of magazines and books.*

When we use **some**, **something**, **somebody**, **someone**, **any**, **anything**, **anybody**, **anyone**, **no**, **nothing**, **nobody**, **no one** as subjects we usually use **There is** as an introduction.

### Exercise 4

Look at the notes about a house and expand the notes to write a fuller description using **There is** and **There are**.

Ground floor: Lounge, kitchen and dining-room.
First floor: 2 bedrooms, bathroom and lavatory.
Second floor: Bedroom and study.
Garden: Greenhouse, toolshed, swimming pool.

# ADJECTIVES 1

**Adjectives with nouns.**
Adjectives are used with nouns to give more information about the noun. Compare sentence **a** with sentence **b**.

*She is wearing a dress.*
*She is wearing a beautiful red dress.*

Adjectives go before nouns, eg:

*A black hat. A wonderful film.*

When more than one adjective is used to describe a noun the adjectives are put in a certain order.

Normally adjectives expressing opinions come before those expressing facts, eg:

*She has a wonderful black cat.*

When we use more than one factual adjective, the adjectives are put in a certain order; the order is usually:

| 1 **Size** | 2 **Age** | 3 **Colour** | 4 **Origin** | 5 **Material** | 6 **Purpose** | |
|---|---|---|---|---|---|---|
| A large | | brown | | leather | travelling | case. |
| A | new | | German | | saloon | car. |
| An | old | blue | | woollen | | overcoat. |
| A small | antique | | | | cigarette | box. |

Usually not more than three factual adjectives are used to describe a noun.

### Exercise 5

Put the adjectives in brackets into the sentence in the correct order.

Example: She is wearing a long green party dress. (party long green)

**1** He lives in a __________ house. (old beautiful Victorian)

**2** I own a __________ bicycle. (racing Italian fantastic)

**3** She has a collection of __________ cups. (china superb coffee)

**4** He often wears __________ glasses on stage. (green large plastic)

**5** I like __________ films. (French old art)

# *Unit 2 Answers*

## EXERCISE 1

**a** His car wasn't stolen last week.
Was his car stolen last week?
Wasn't his car stolen last week?

**b** The protesters weren't arrested.
Were the protesters arrested?
Weren't the protesters arrested?

**c** President Kennedy wasn't assassinated by one person.
Was President Kennedy assassinated by one person?
Wasn't President Kennedy assassinated by one person?

## EXERCISE 2

Coffee wasn't being served.
Was coffee being served?
Wasn't coffee being served?

## EXERCISE 3

**1** got
**2** went
**3** looked
**4** was shining
**5** saw
**6** was
**7** had
**8** dressed
**9** drank
**10** left
**11** ran
**12** were waiting
**13** were talking
**14** were standing
**15** arrived
**16** got
**17** was
**18** was
**19** was being repaired
**20** looked
**21** hoped
**22** was
**23** arrived
**24** noticed
**25** was working
**26** came
**27** said
**28** was looking

## EXERCISE 4

On the ground floor there is a lounge, a kitchen and a dining room.
On the first floor there are two bedrooms, a bathroom and a lavatory.
On the second floor there is a bedroom and a study.
In the garden there is a greenhouse, a toolshed and a swimming pool.

## EXERCISE 5

**1** He lives in a beautiful old Victorian house.
**2** I own a fantastic Italian racing bicycle.
**3** She has a collection of superb china coffee cups.
**4** He often wears large green plastic glasses on stage.
**5** I like old French art films.

# WAYS OF EXPRESSING THE FUTURE

There are several ways of expressing the future. As we are only able to guess about or predict the future, our choice of which form we use depends partly on how certain we are about something and partly on our evidence for our certainty. In some of the explanations given here, different future forms are used together; do not at first try to work out the differences; just concentrate on the forms and their uses.

## PRESENT PROGRESSIVE ACTIVE/PASSIVE

### FORM

This is exactly the same as when it is used to express present actions, see **Spotlight on Language p. 147**.

### USES

The present progressive is used to express the future when we have some evidence about the future event we are describing. Look at these examples:

*I'm playing football this weekend.*

The decision was already made some time before, for example, the captain of the football team asked you to play and you accepted the invitation.

*I'm going to London tomorrow.*

Again the decision is made. For some reason you want to go to London, to see a friend, to go shopping, etc.

*England are playing Switzerland tonight.*

You know this because it was in the newspapers or you heard it from a friend or on the radio, etc.

The uses are the same in the negative, interrogative and negative interrogative. Look at these examples:

*I am not going to Jane's party.*

The decision is made either because you cannot or do not want to go to the party or you did not get an invitation.

*What are you doing tonight?*

You are asking about any plans your friend has for the evening.

*Aren't you eating at your brother's tonight?*

You assume that your friend is eating at his brother's and are seeking confirmation.

The present progressive when used in the passive as a future form also reflects plans already made, eg:

*The team is being announced tomorrow.*

## (BE) GOING TO

### FORM

| | | | | | |
|---|---|---|---|---|---|
| | Pronoun/noun + primary auxiliary (be) + going to + infinitive | | | | |
| Affirmative | He | is | | going to | fall. |
| | Pronoun/noun + primary auxiliary + not + going to + infinitive | | | | |
| Negative | She | is | not | going to | come. |
| | Primary auxiliary + pronoun/noun + going to + infinitive | | | | |
| Interrogative | Are | you | | going to | finish soon? |
| | Primary auxiliary + pronoun/noun + not + going to + infinitive | | | | |
| Negative interrogative | Is | he | not | going to | pay? |
| Contraction | Isn't | he | | going to | pay? |

## USE

The **going to** form of the future is most often used when the decision about what we are going to do or what is going to happen is supported by evidence present at the time of speaking or a decision arrived at by the time of speaking. Look at the examples given for the form of **going to** in more detail:

*He's going to fall.*

Imagine we are watching somebody climbing a tree. He is having problems and we think that the person is likely to fall.

*She's not going to come.*

You are waiting for a friend. She is now half an hour late. You know she is usually on time or that it was not certain that she was able to come, so you think that she is not coming. Look at these sentences and think of reasons behind them.

**a** It is going to rain.
**b** I'm going to go home now.
**c** He's going to fail his driving test.
**d** Aren't you going to eat your pudding?
**e** I think the police are going to arrest him.

# (BE) GOING TO – PASSIVE

## FORM

| | Pronoun/noun + primary auxiliary + going to be + past participle | | | |
|---|---|---|---|---|
| Affirmative | The museum | is | going to be | repainted. |

The negative, interrogative and negative interrogative are formed in the same way as the present progressive passive.

## USES

The **going to** form of the passive indicates something that is going to be done to something or someone.

**Exercise 1**

For practice turn the above into the other forms.

# WILL/SHALL

## FORM

| | | | | |
|---|---|---|---|---|
| | Pronoun/noun + modal auxiliary (will) + infinitive | | | |
| Affirmative | She | will | arrive | tomorrow. |
| | Pronoun/noun + modal auxiliary (will) + not + infinitive | | | |
| Negative | They | will | not | like the cold. |
| | Modal auxiliary + pronoun/noun + infinitive | | | |
| Interrogative | Will | they | bring | their children? |
| | Modal auxiliary + pronoun/noun + not + infinitive | | | |
| Negative interrogative | Will | he | not | meet them? |
| Contraction | Won't | he | | meet them? |

**NB**
**Will** is usually used for all persons nowadays. **Shall** is however sometimes used for the first person singular and plural usually in formal letters.

**Will** contracts to **'ll** as does **shall**. **Will not** contracts to **won't**, **shall not** contracts to **shan't**.

The passive is formed according to rules previously given. An example is:

*Your car will be repaired by tomorrow.*

## USES

Sometimes the **will** form is the first future form that learners of English are taught or the one they think of as the most important. In fact other forms of the future are more common so try to think about what you really want to express before choosing which future form you use.

The **will/shall** form most often expresses a person's immediate reaction to a situation and the action they will take. Usually little or no pre-planning is involved, eg:

*It's cold in here. I'll put the fire on.*

In the above example the speaker is expressing his/her immediate reaction to something that happened.

The **will/shall** form is also used when the speaker thinks that something is so certain to happen in the future that neither he nor anybody else can alter it. Look at the following example:

*I'll be thirty-one next year.*

# DIFFERENCES BETWEEN THE FUTURE FORMS

It is often difficult to see the differences between the forms when we just look at sentences without knowing the context, but let's look at these examples:

*I'm going to the doctor's tomorrow.*
*I'm going to go to the doctor's tomorrow.*
*I'll go to the doctor's tomorrow.*

In the first example the speaker has evidence for his statement almost certainly because the appointment is already made.

In the second example the speaker is expressing a decision made in the past but maybe an appointment is not yet arranged.

In the third example the speaker is reacting to an immediate situation; pehaps he is in pain or worried about something but it is certainly a spontaneous decision and no appointment is arranged.

### Exercise 2

Put the verbs in brackets into the future form you think is correct.

William and Mary return home after an evening at the cinema.

W: Gosh! It's cold in here.
M: You're right. I (1. *turn*) the heating on. Oh! by the way, I (2. *make*) a coffee. Do you want one?
W: No thanks, I think I (3. *have*) a whisky instead.

The phone rings.

W: I (4. *answer*) it.
M: Thanks, I (5. *bring*) your drink through.
W: Mary, it's Bill. (6. *do*) we anything tomorrow night?
M: Well, we (7. *fetch*) the car from the garage, but we (8. *be*) back by 6.00.
W: Fine. Bill (9. *go*) out to a restaurant and wants us to join him.
M: Great! I (10. *enjoy*) that.
W: (To Bill.) That's fine we (11. *meet*) you at 7.00 at the Royal Oak.
M: Which restaurant (12. *go*) we to?
W: The Tatler.
M: (13. *Bring*) Bill his girlfriend?
W: I imagine so. Well, I think I (14. *go*) to bed now. (15. *come*) you?
M: No, I think I (16. *watch*) the late news first.

# ADJECTIVES 2 (COMPARATIVES and SUPERLATIVES)

## FORM

The comparative of an adjective is formed by either adding **-er** to the adjective or by putting the word **more** in front of it. Usually short words add **-er** and longer ones take the word **more**.

The superlative is formed in a similar way but **-est** or **most** are used.

**NB**

**1** All one-syllable adjectives (with the exception of **good**, **bad** and **far**) have the **-er** form for the comparative and **-est** for the superlative. If the adjective ends in **-e** then we just add **-r** or **-st**. For example:

*late later latest*
*ripe riper ripest*
*safe safer safest*

If the adjective ends in a vowel followed by a consonant then the consonant is doubled before adding **-er** or **-est**, eg:

*fat fatter fattest*
*thin thinner thinnest*
*wet wetter wettest*
*red redder reddest*

The following common adjectives are irregular:

| | | |
|---|---|---|
| *good* | *better* | *best* |
| *bad* | *worse* | *worst* |
| *far* | *farther* | *farthest* |
| *far* | *further* | *furthest* |

**1** **Old** when used to describe a brother/sister or son/daughter has an additional irregular form, **elder eldest**.

*My elder brother.*
*Her eldest daughter.*

**2** The majority of adjectives with two syllables take **more** and **most**. Two syllable adjectives ending in **-y** drop the **-y** and add **-ier** or **-iest**, for example:

| | | |
|---|---|---|
| *happy* | *happier* | *happiest* |
| *lucky* | *luckier* | *luckiest* |
| *lovely* | *lovelier* | *loveliest* |

There are some two syllable adjectives which can either add **-er**, **-est** or take **more** and **most**, eg **clever**. You will always be correct if you use **more** and **most** with these adjectives.

**3** With adjectives of three or more syllables it is always correct to use **more** and **most**.

*expensive more expensive most expensive*

## USE

Comparing things which are equal.
Here we use **as . . . as**.

*She is as clever as he is.*
*I'm as tall as you are.*

Comparing things which are not equal. Here we have a choice of different ways of saying the same thing. Look at these different ways of comparing the size of France and Britain.

*France is bigger than Britain.*
*Britain is smaller than France.*
*Britain is not as big as France.*
*Britain is not so big as France.*

They all mean the same and are all equally correct.

**Less** means the opposite of **more**.

*I am less ruthless than my brother. = My brother is more ruthless than I am.*

The comparative form is only used to compare two things. To compare more than two things, use the superlative form: **-est**, **most** or **least**.

*Everest is the highest mountain in the world.*
*The Queen is the richest woman in Britain.*
*She's the most attractive person I know.*
*He's the least intelligent person in the class.*

**Exercise 3**

Look at the information given on the next page about four students in the same class and make as many sentences as possible using comparatives and superlatives. Remember also to use equal comparatives when appropriate.

| Name | John | Mary | Julia | Paul |
|---|---|---|---|---|
| Age | 17 | 17 | 16 | 18 |
| Height | 1.82 m | 1.62 m | 1.59 m | 1.87 m |
| Weight | 67 kg | 60 kg | 60 kg | 73 kg |
| Marks for: | | | | |
| English | 84 | 87 | 63 | 54 |
| Mathematics | 73 | 73 | 82 | 31 |

# *Unit 3 Answers*

## EXERCISE 1

The museum is not going to be repainted.
Is the museum going to be repainted?
Isn't the museum going to be repainted?

## EXERCISE 2

**1** I'll turn
**2** I'm going to make/I'm making
**3** I'll have
**4** I'll answer
**5** I'll bring
**6** Are we doing
**7** are fetching
**8** we will
**9** is going
**10** I'll enjoy
**11** we will
**12** are we going
**13** Is Bill bringing
**14** I'll go
**15** Are you coming
**16** I'll watch

## EXERCISE 3

There are many different sentences that can be made. The following are a few examples.
Paul is older than Julia.
Mary is the same age as John.
Julia is shorter than Mary.
Paul is heavier than John.
John is better at English than Paul.

UNIT 4

# INTRODUCTORY SUBJECT: 'It'

In **Spotlight on Language p. 153** we looked at the use of **There** as an introductory subject. We also often use **It** as an introductory subject when the main subject is a **that** clause or an infinitive. Although it is not incorrect to start with an infinitive or **that** clause it is more usual to use an introductory subject. Let's look at some examples:

*It's a pity you weren't able to come to the party.*
*It's obvious that she doesn't like me.*
*It was discovered that the painting was missing.*
*It's very nice to meet you.*

We often use the introductory subject **it** with passive constructions because the identity of the person is not important or not actually known:

*Doctors say that smoking is bad for the health.*
*It is said that smoking is bad for the health.*

We also use **it** when we state our own opinion and want to make it sound more general. For example:

*It's a good thing that he is not here.*
*It's useless to study grammar.*

# CONDITION

Most of life is ruled by conditions. Things that we want to do are sometimes controlled by factors over which we have no control, so when we express something we are thinking of doing we often mention the conditions for doing it. The words we most often use to express conditions are **if**, **unless**, **so long as**, **provided that**, **in case**, **on condition that**, **whatever**, **whether . . . or**. Because we often state conditions when expressing plans etc. the expressions we use usually consist of two clauses, the **main** clause and the **if**-clause. These sentences are called conditional sentences and there are three types in English. This unit looks at the first one.

# THE FIRST CONDITIONAL

## FORM

The first conditional consists of two clauses, the **main** clause and the **if**-clause. The **main** clause usually uses the **will/shall** form of the future, see **Spotlight on Language p. 156** and the **if**-clause uses the present simple, see **Spotlight on Language p. 145**. It usually does not matter which clause comes first. Look at this example:

| **Main clause** | **If-clause** |
|---|---|
| We'll go for a walk | if it is a nice day. |
| **If-clause** | **Main clause** |
| If it is a nice day | we'll go for a walk. |

Sometimes both the **main** clause and the **if**-clause use the present simple tense. This is to express scientific facts or something we know from our own experience. Look at this example:

*If you freeze water it turns to ice.*

In this example **if** means *every time* or *when*.

## USE

We use the first conditional to express the conditions for something to happen or not happen. It is sometimes called the probable conditional because we expect the event to happen if the conditions are satisfied.

In addition to **if** we can use other condition words and expressions. We will now look at some of the most usual ones.

**Unless**.

**Unless** is often used instead of **if not**. Look at this pair of sentences.

*We'll go out if it doesn't rain. = We'll go out unless it rains.*

**Whether** and **whether . . . or . . .**

These expressions are usually used when we want to express alternatives.

*I don't know whether I'll come to the party (or not).*

**Provided that**, **so/as long as**, **in case**, **on condition that**, **whatever**.

All these expressions can be used in conditional sentences. The following examples show you how they are used.

*Take your umbrella with you in case it rains.*
*Provided that you return it by 10.00 you can borrow my car.*
*I'll lend you £5 so/as long as you give it back on Monday.*
*I'll let you stay for the night on condition that you don't smoke in the house.*
*Whatever the weather we'll go for a walk.*

**Exercise 1**

Expand these clauses into first conditional sentences using the conditions given in brackets.

Example: We'll go on holiday. (enough money)
We'll go on holiday if we have enough money.

**1** I'll give you £100. (stop smoking)
**2** We'll go to the concert. (get a ticket)
**3** I won't see you. (back by 10.00)
**4** She won't come to your party. (apologise)
**5** You won't get a pay increase. (work harder)

# *Unit 4 Answers*

## EXERCISE 1

**1** I'll give you £100 if you stop smoking.
**2** We'll go to the concert if we get a ticket.
**3** I won't see you unless you are back by 10.00.
**4** She won't come to your party unless you apologise.
**5** You won't get a pay increase unless you work harder.

UNIT
5

# PRESENT PERFECT SIMPLE ACTIVE

## FORM

| | | | | | |
|---|---|---|---|---|---|
| Affirmative | Pronoun/noun + primary auxiliary (have) + past participle | | | | |
| | I | have | | seen | him. |
| Negative | Pronoun/noun + primary auxiliary (have) + not + past participle | | | | |
| | I | have | not | seen | him. |
| Interrogative | Primary auxiliary + pronoun/noun + past participle | | | | |
| | Have | you | | seen | him? |
| Negative interrogative | Primary auxiliary + pronoun/noun + not + past participle | | | | |
| | Have | you | not | seen | him? |
| Contraction | Haven't | you | | seen | him? |

**She has**, **he has** and **it has** contract to **she's**, **he's** and **it's**. Be careful not to confuse these contractions with the contractions for the present simple of the main verb **to be** and for the present progressive of verbs. To tell whether it is a contraction for **is** or **has** you have to look at the words which follow the contractions.

**Exercise 1**

Look at the following sentences and decide what **'s** stands for: **is** or **has**.

**1** He's hungry.
**2** He's coming tomorrow.
**3** She's bought a new car.
**4** It's a lovely day.
**5** It's starting to rain.
**6** It's started to rain.

# PRESENT PERFECT SIMPLE PASSIVE

## FORM

| | | | |
|---|---|---|---|
| | Pronoun/noun + primary auxiliary + past participle | | |
| Affirmative | Your car | has been | stolen. |

The negative, interrogative and negative interrogatives are formed in the same way as the other passives already introduced. See **Spotlight on Language p. 146**.

**Exercise 2**

For practice turn the above sentence into those forms.

# PRESENT PERFECT SIMPLE ACTIVE and PASSIVE

## USE

The present perfect simple is a tense which learners often find difficult as there are so many uses. The most important thing to remember is that when we use it we are always looking back from the present, and if we are expressing something about ourselves it can be to any point in our lifetime, eg:

*I've always loved chocolate.*

If we are expressing something about someone or something else it can be longer than our lifetime, but the 'someone or something else' must still be alive today, eg:

*My grandmother has always been a communist.*

Not:

*Shakespeare has written some good plays.*

Nearly always, however, it is something that happens now (at present) which causes us to think about the past. The following examples are in pairs. The first of each pair contains the reason why we look back into the past and therefore the reason that we choose the present perfect. In some of the sentences you will see words like **just**, **already**, **since**, **for**, **ever**, **never**, **yet** and **before**, which often indicate the use of the present perfect.

A: *I went to see 'The Godfather' at the cinema last night.*
B: *Oh! I've seen that, it's a very good film.*

A: *I'm looking for Jack Brown.*
B: *He's just left.*

A: *We stayed in the Hilton Hotel in London.*
B: *What's it like? I've never been there.*

A: *Please give me your homework now.*
B: *I'm sorry, I haven't finished it yet.*

A: *Do you want some breakfast?*
B: *No thanks, I've already eaten.*

A: *Manchester United were beaten last night.*
B: *I know. They haven't won for three weeks.*

A: *How is your sister?*
B: *I don't know. I haven't seen her since Easter.*

A: *I can't find my car keys.*
B: *Have you looked in your raincoat pocket?*

A: *Are the Browns coming to the party.*
B: *I don't know. Haven't they replied yet?*

Having looked at some examples of the present perfect simple let's look more closely at when and how it is used and the words and expressions it is most often used with.

It is used to describe things which started in the past and have continued up to now or have only very recently stopped. When the present perfect is used like this, it usually takes one of the following time expressions:

### For

**For** is used to tell us how long an action has lasted.

*I've known her for three weeks.*

With the above expression there is nothing to indicate that the action will not continue in the future.

### Since

**Since** is used to tell us when an action started. The sentence used to explain **for** can be rewritten using **since**:

*I've known her since March 1st.* (it's now March 22nd)

Again it is possible that the actions will continue in the future.

### Other time expressions

There are many other time expressions that are used to convey something that started in the past and have continued up to now, eg:

*I've always loved wine.*
*I've lived here all my life.*
*I've recently started yoga.*

All the examples we have looked at so far have involved one continuous action but the present perfect can also be used to express an action which started in the past and has been repeated a number of times up to now, eg:

*I've often eaten in that restaurant.*
*She's telephoned six times since lunchtime.*

The present perfect simple is also used to express actions and events which happened in the past but are now finished, but only when it is because the action or event which we are describing is relevant to the present situation we are in. It is often used in this way when we are telling someone about a recent piece of news or giving them a piece of information they may not have heard before. Here are some examples:

*My sister's had a baby.*
*Mark has broken his arm.*
*I've passed my driving test.*
*The Prime Minister has resigned.*

**Words and expressions often used with the present perfect**

**Just** usually means a moment, a few seconds or a few minutes ago. It is used with the present perfect to express an action or event that has happened in the very recent past, eg:

*I've just finished work.*

**Already** is used with the present perfect to indicate that an action or event has happened, eg:

*She's already gone.*

**Yet** is used with the present perfect to ask about whether an action or event has happened or to express that an action or event has not happened up to now.

*Have you met the new boss yet?*
*I haven't made the dinner yet.*

**Other expressions:**
**Still**, **before**, **ever**, and **never**.

*He still hasn't given me my camera back.*
*Have you eaten here before?*
*Have you ever been to Italy?*
*She's never met my parents.*

# PRESENT PERFECT PROGRESSIVE (ACTIVE)

## FORM

| | | | | |
|---|---|---|---|---|
| | Pronoun/noun + perfect participle + present participle | | | |
| Affirmative | You | have been | working | very hard |
| | Pronoun/noun + perfect participle + not + present participle | | | |
| Negative | You | have not been | working | very hard |
| | Perfect participle + pronoun/noun + present participle | | | |
| Interrogative | Have | you been working | | very hard? |
| | Perfect participle + pronoun/noun + not + present participle | | | |
| Negative interrogative | Have you not been working very hard? | | | |
| Contraction | Haven't | you | been working | very hard? |

Note the present progressive passive is exceptionally rarely used and is not worth dealing with.

## USE

The present perfect progressive like the present perfect (see Spotlight on Language 5) is also used when we are looking back from the present but it is usually used to express more temporary actions. Look at this example.

*I've now waited over a month for my results.*
*I've been waiting in the cold for my flatmate to turn up.*

The first sentence uses the present perfect because the period is of quite a long duration. The second sentence indicates a shorter period in the recent past.

# PAST SIMPLE and PRESENT PERFECT

Although the only real way to learn the differences between these two tenses is by practice, the following 'rules' may help:

The present perfect is almost never used with definite time expressions such as: **at 6 o'clock**, **in March**, **during August**, **yesterday**, **last week**, **four years ago**, etc. With these expressions use the past simple.

When speaking or writing about a sequence of events always use the past simple.

When the action or event has no connection with the present use the past simple not the present perfect.

**Exercise 3**

In this exercise expand the sentences putting the verbs in capital letters into either the past simple or present perfect.

**1** I (*GO*) to bed at ten o'clock last night.
**2** How often (*EAT*) you at this restaurant?
**3** Where (*BE*) you at lunchtime?
**4** The boss has been looking for you for ten minutes. Where (*BE*) you?
**5** Who is the girl in the red dress? I (*SEE*) not her before.
**6** I don't want any lunch. I (*EAT*) already.
**7** I'm afraid you (*MISS*) John, he just (*GO*).
**8** We (*DECIDE*) not yet where to go for our holidays.
**9** (*HEAR*) you Mary is getting married?
**10** (*GET*) you 'The Times' yesterday?

# *Unit 5 Answers*

## EXERCISE 1

**1** is
**2** is
**3** has
**4** is
**5** is
**6** has

## EXERCISE 2

Your car has not been stolen.
Has your car been stolen?
Hasn't your car been stolen?

## EXERCISE 3

**1** went
**2** have you eaten
**3** were
**4** have you been
**5** haven't seen
**6** have already eaten
**7** have missed
has just gone
**8** haven't decided
**9** Have you heard
**10** Did you get

UNIT
6

# MODALS

Primary auxiliaries **be**, **do** and **have** are used to form different tenses with main verbs (see **Spotlight on Language Unit 1**). Modal auxiliaries are also used with main verbs, but do not alter the tense of the main verb. Instead they express something about the opinion of the speaker or ask for the opinion of the listener, including degrees of certainty, eg How certain is it that an event or action will happen? and degrees of necessity, eg How important is it that an event or action happens? Before looking at the form and use of individual modal auxiliaries let's first look at a group of them that share a certain amount of things in common:

*can may must shall will*
*could might should would*

They all come before the main verb. They are not used together. They do not change form, ie the way that they are used to form negatives, interrogatives, and negative interrogatives is identical.

## FORM

When they are used with main verbs the main verb is an infinitive without **to**. There are four types of infinitive:

| | | | | | |
|---|---|---|---|---|---|
| Present | Come, speak, walk, etc. | | | | |
| Progressive | Be coming, be speaking, be walking, etc. and similarly for the other progressive tenses. Have been coming, etc. | | | | |
| Perfect | Have come, have spoken, have walked, etc. | | | | |
| Passive | Be spoken, be walked, be seen, etc. | | | | |
| Affirmative | Pronoun/noun + modal auxiliary + infinitive | | | | |
| | She | can | | speak | French. |

| | | | | | |
|---|---|---|---|---|---|
| Negative | Pronoun/noun + modal auxiliary + not + infinitive | | | | |
| | She | can | not | speak | French. |
| Interrogative | Modal auxiliary + pronoun/noun + infinitive | | | | |
| | Can | she | | speak | French? |
| Negative interrogative | Modal auxiliary + pronoun/noun + not + infinitive | | | | |
| | Can | she | not | speak | French? |
| Contraction | Can't | she | | speak | French? |

All the other modal auxiliaries mentioned above follow the same form, eg:

*She could speak French.*
*She may speak French.*
*She might not speak French.*
*Must she speak French?*

*I shan't speak French.*
*Shouldn't she speak French?*
*Will she speak French?*
*She wouldn't speak French.*

## USES

The most important thing to remember about all modals is that we use them to express our present opinion or ask somebody else their present opinion.

### **Can** and **could**

Although **can** and **could** have many different meanings, they all indicate a degree of possibility with **can** usually expressing a more certain possibility and **could** a less certain possibility.

**1** **Can** means to be able to

*I can wash up*

This means:

I know how to wash up

**Could** expresses the ability to do something in the past.

*I could play the piano when I was seven.*

This means:

I knew how to play the piano when I was seven.

**2** **Can** and **could** are also used to express future possibility:

*I can help you tomorrow.*

This means:

It is certainly possible for me to help you tomorrow.

*I could help you tomorrow.*

This means:

It is not absolutely certain that it is possible for me to help you tomorrow.

**3** **Can** and **could** are also used to ask permission.

*Can I leave early today?*

This means:

Is it possible for me to leave early?

*Could I leave early today?*

This means almost the same as the sentence above but is used when the relationship is more 'distant', ie somebody we know but probably not a close friend.

**4** **Can** and **could** are also used with requests.

*Can you help me with my homework?*

This means:

Is it possible for you to help me with my homework?

*Could you help me with my homework?*

More distant as above.

**5** **Can** and **could** are also used with offers.

*I can repair your bicycle for you.*

This means:

*It is possible for me to repair your bicycle if you want me to.*

*I could repair your bicycle for you.*

This again means nearly the same as above but we think it is less likely that the person will want us to or that we are less sure that we want to do it.

**6** **Can** and **could** are also used to discuss the possibility of something.

*It could be gold.*

Here we are looking at something and speculating about what it is made of.

*It can't be gold.*

In this case we have decided that it is certainly not gold, possibly because it is not heavy enough.
**NB Can** is not used in the affirmative for this use, eg *'It can be gold'* is wrong.

### **May** and **might**

**May** and **might** are sometimes used in very similar ways to **can** and **could** and when they are, the differences between **may** and **might** are similar to those between **can** and **could**. Let's first look at the differences.

*I can come tomorrow* and *I could come tomorrow* indicate the degrees of possibility for the speaker to come tomorrow. It is as if the speaker has already made a decision.

*I may come tomorrow* and *I might come tomorrow* again indicates degrees of possibility but the speaker is indicating that he has not yet made a decision, with **might** being even less certain than **may**.

## USES

**1** **May** is used for permission in very much the same way as **can**. Some people think it is more polite but it is not used so often as it was in the past.

*May I leave early tonight? = Can I leave early tonight?*

**2** **May** and **might** are also used when discussing the possibility of something that is still unknown.

*It may rain.*
*It might be made of gold.*

### **Must**, **have to**, and **have got to**

Although **have to** and **have got to** were not included in the list of modals they are often used in the same way and are similar in meaning to **must**. However their form does change so we will study it here.

## FORM

| | | |
|---|---|---|
| Affirmative | He has to leave now. | He has got to leave now. |
| Negative | He doesn't have to leave now. | He hasn't got to leave now. |
| Interrogative | Does he have to leave now? | Has he got to leave now? |
| Negative/interrogative | Doesn't he have to leave now? | Hasn't he got to leave now? |

## USES

**1** **Must**, **have to** and **have got to** are all used to express necessity, eg:

*I must catch the 7 o'clock train.*

This can be either because I have decided that I want to catch that train and therefore it is personally necessary or because, for example, I have a meeting and that is the only train that will get me there on time.

When we used the second person the difference between **must** and **have (got) to** is clearer.

*You must telephone your mother.*

This means that I find it important that you telephone your mother.

*You have to telephone your mother.*

This means, for example, that you have received a message from the person's mother and that it is important that he telephones her.

**Must**, **have to** and **have got to**, although having similar meanings in the affirmative have very different meanings in the negative. Look at these sentences:

*You mustn't tell him.*
*You don't have to tell him.*

The first sentence means:

*It is important that you do not tell him.*

The second sentence means:

*It is not important that you tell him.*

When we express a necessity in the past we use **had to** for both **must** and **have to**, eg:

*I had to get up early this morning.*

When we want to express a necessity in the future there are three ways of doing it.

*You must see the doctor tomorrow.*
*You have to see the doctor tomorrow.*
*You'll have to see the doctor tomorrow.*

The first sentence means I think it is a necessity.

The second sentence means it is a necessity because, for example, you have made an appointment.

The third sentence expresses the speaker's immediate reaction to something, eg the person is coughing very badly. Compare this with the **will** form of the future, see **Spotlight on Language p. 156**.

**2** **Must**, **have to** and **have got to** are also used to express near certainty about something based on the evidence we have, eg you see a large animal in Africa on TV and can't see what it is.

*It must be an elephant.*

### **Mustn't** and **needn't**

**Need** is sometimes confused with **mustn't**, eg:

*You mustn't tell anybody where I live.*
*You needn't tell anybody where I live.*

In the first sentence we mean:

*It is necessary **not** to tell anybody where I live.*

In the second sentence we mean:

*It is **not** necessary to tell anybody where I live.*

**Shall** see **Spotlight on Language p. 156**

### **Should** and **ought to**

We often use **ought to** in a similar way to **should**.

**Should** and **ought to** are used to express necessity and obligation. They do not express such strong necessity as **must** and **have to**, but more 'It is/is not a good idea to do something.'

Look at these sentences:

*I should go home now.*
*I ought to go home now.*

The meaning is very similar but in the first sentence you are expressing the fact that you have decided it is a good idea to go home. In the second sentence you are expressing the fact that there is a reason for going home, eg you are late and somebody is waiting for you.

**Will** see **Spotlight on Language p. 156**

### **Would**

We know that **will** is used when a speaker reacts immediately to a situation. **Would** is used when a speaker is expressing what his reaction is likely to be if a certain situation occurred. Look at these sentences:

*I'd like to see you tomorrow.*

The speaker is saying that the way he feels now is that if you are available tomorrow he wants to see you.

*I wouldn't want anything to happen to John.*

The speaker is saying that if anything happened to John he would not be happy.

*I would be very surprised if he passed his driving test.*

The speaker is saying that he does not expect him to pass but if he does it will be a surprise.

## USES

1 **Would** is often used in polite requests.

*Would you open the window, please?*

2 **Would** is also used with offers.

*Would you like a drink?*

3 **Would** is often used to express past habits.

*I would often go to the seaside when I was young.*

4 **Would** is used in second conditional sentences.

# THE SECOND CONDITIONAL

## FORM

The first conditional sentences in **Spotlight on Language p. 160** showed that they are formed by two clauses, the **main** clause and the **-if** clause. With the second conditional the **main** clause uses **would** and the **-if** clause uses **the past tense** as a conditional. Either clause can start the sentence:

*If you worked harder you'd pass the examination.*
*You'd pass the examination if you worked harder.*

**NB** Sometimes **were** is used instead of **was** after 2nd and 3rd persons, specially in more formal situations.

*If he were rich he'd buy a house in France.*

## USE

The first conditional is sometimes called the probable conditional. The second conditional is sometimes called the possible conditional because it expresses things that we do not expect to happen. Compare these two sentences:

*If I meet the Prime Minister I'll ask about her plans for Education.*
*If I met the Prime Minister I'd ask about her plans for Education.*

The first sentence might be said by a Member of Parliament who has a good chance of meeting the Prime Minister.

The second sentence might be said by an ordinary member of public who is unlikely to meet the Prime Minister.

The second conditional is also used to sound more polite. Look at these sentences:

*Is it alright if I turn the television off?*
*Would it be alright if I turned the television off?*

The first sentence can sound too direct; the second sentence is politer.

### Exercise 1

Expand these clauses into second conditional sentences using the conditions given in brackets.

**1** I'd give up work. (enough money)
**2** You wouldn't have a cough. (give up smoking)
**3** She wouldn't go out with him. (like him)
**4** You'd catch your train. (leave now)
**5** Britain would be a wonderful country to live in. (rain so much)

## ADVERBS: COMPARATIVE AND SUPERLATIVES

Most comparative and superlative adverbs are formed with **more** and **most**

*Could you speak more clearly?*
*She sings most beautifully.*

The following adverbs, however, form comparatives and superlatives with **-er** and **-est**.

| | | |
|---|---|---|
| Early | earlier | earliest |
| Fast | faster | fastest |
| Hard | harder | hardest |
| Long | longer | longest |

In addition, the following adverbs have irregular forms:

| | | |
|---|---|---|
| badly | worse | worst |
| far | further | furthest |
| | farther | farthest |
| little | less | least |
| much | more | most |
| well | better | best |

# *Unit 6 Answers*

## EXERCISE 1

**1** I'd give up work if I had enough money.
**2** You wouldn't have a cough if you gave up smoking.
**3** She wouldn't go out with him if she didn't like him.
**4** You'd catch your train if you left now.
**5** Britain would be a wonderful country to live in if it didn't rain so much.

UNIT 7

# SO DO I, NEITHER DO I, ETC.

## FORM

| | | | |
|---|---|---|---|
| Affirmative | So + auxiliary + pronoun/noun | | |
| | So | was | I. |
| Negative | Neither/nor + auxiliary + pronoun/noun | | |
| | Neither/nor | did | I. |

The auxiliary used is usually the one in the clause/sentence with which we are agreeing.

*'I was late this morning.' 'So was I.'*
*'I must go to the bank.' 'So must I.'*
*'I don't like beer.' 'Neither/nor do I.'*
*'I haven't finished my homework.' 'Neither/nor have I.'*

If there is no auxiliary before the main verb we use the appropriate form of **do**.

*'I love classical music.' 'So do I.'*
*'I saw her yesterday.' 'So did I.'*

**NB** Be careful to think about what contractions stand for before you decide which auxiliary to use.

*'He's got two brothers.' 'So have I.'*
*'She's going to the cinema.' 'So am I.'*

Be careful with **have** when it is used as a main verb. If another verb can be used instead of **have** it is usual to use the auxiliary **do** rather than **have**.

*'I had (ate) breakfast at 7.00.' 'So did I.'*
*'I had (received) a letter this morning.' 'So did I.'*

## USE

We use the above expressions to mean **also** or **too**. They are short ways of saying that you have the same opinion as the speaker or have had the same experiences.

### Exercise 2

For each of the sentences use either **so**, **neither/nor** + appropriate auxiliary to produce short responses.

**1** I'm not going to his party.
**2** I hate parties.
**3** I won't give him a present.
**4** I can't stand pop music.
**5** I should go home now.
**6** I might go out later.
**7** First I must have something to eat.
**8** I only had a sandwich for lunch.
**9** Right, I'm going now.
**10** I'll try to arrive at work early tomorrow.

# THE GERUND

When we use the **-ing** form as a noun it is called a gerund. Just like other nouns the gerund can be used as a subject or object:

*Exercise is good for you.*
*I like tennis.*

Now look at these sentences which use gerunds:

*Swimming is good for you.*
*I like skiing.*

# THE GERUND USED AFTER VERBS

## FORM and USE

Usually when one verb is followed by another verb the second verb is in the infinitive.

*I want to see him.*
*He expected to pass the examination.*

Some verbs, however, are followed by a gerund and not an infinitive. This list of the most common ones may be helpful to refer to:

| admit | appreciate | avoid | consider | delay |
|---|---|---|---|---|
| deny | detest | dislike | enjoy | escape |
| fancy | finish | imagine | mind | miss |
| postpone | practise | regret | risk | suggest |

These are examples using the verbs in the first column.

*He admitted stealing my cheque book.*
*She denied killing her husband.*
*I fancy going to the cinema.*
*The government has postponed making a decision until next month.*

**Exercise 3**

For practice make sentences using the verbs in the other columns.

There are other times when we use a gerund. The most important ones are:

1 **After a preposition**
The gerund is used after prepositions both when a preposition is used on its own and when it is used with a verb.

*We must eat before going to the cinema.*
*I'm looking forward to seeing you.*
*A lot of accidents are caused by drunken driving.*

There are many prepositional verbs and phrasal verbs in English. Remember that if they have a preposition they are followed by a gerund. The following are very common examples:

*He apologised for being late.*
*I'm not interested in going to discos.*
*I'm trying to give up smoking.*

2 **When used with a passive meaning**
With the verbs **need**, **want**, **require**, and **deserve** the gerund is often used to indicate a passive meaning, ie what should be done not who should do it.

*The windows need cleaning.*
*His house wants repairing.*

**Exercise 4**

Look at these sentences and decide if they are correct or not. If they are not correct, write down the correct form.

1 I don't want to play tennis.
2 I enjoy to play tennis.
3 He suggested to go for a walk.
4 I'm fond of listening to the radio.
5 Do you mind to help me for a minute?
6 Do you regret not going to university?
7 Before to start the meal please wash your hands.
8 Your shirt needs to iron.
9 He needs to see the doctor.
10 They missed to see the film.

# PAST PROGRESSIVE and PAST SIMPLE

## FORM

See **Spotlight on Language pp. 150–151**.

## USES (2)

The past progressive and past simple are often used together in sentences. The past progressive usually refers to the longer action and the past simple to a shorter action which happened during the longer action or which interrupted it:

*When I arrived she was still working.*
*He telephoned while I was having a shower.*

Sometimes either **while** or **when** may be used but it is always correct to use **while** with the past progressive and **when** with the past simple.

**Exercise 1**

Combine these pairs of sentences to make one longer sentence, using **while** or **when**.

1 I was living in Canterbury. Kennedy was assassinated.
2 I met her. She was studying law.
3 She fell asleep. He was reading.
4 The road was being repaired. The accident happened.
5 The lights went out. We were eating.

# PAST PERFECT SIMPLE

## FORM

| | Pronoun/noun + auxiliary (had) + past participle | | |
|---|---|---|---|
| Affirmative | I | had | heard. |

The negative, interrogative and negative interrogative are formed in the same ways as for the present perfect except that the auxiliary **had** is used instead of **have**. See **Spotlight on Language p. 162**.

*It had already been repaired.*
*I hadn't been told.*

The passive is also formed in the same way as for the present perfect but using **had**, see **Spotlight on Language p. 162**.

**NB I had** contracts to **I'd** and **I had not** to **I hadn't**.

## USES

The uses of the past perfect are like those of the present perfect in every way except that the time referred to instead of being before the present, is before a particular point already in the past.

**1** When we talk about two actions in the past the past perfect is used to refer to the earlier action. We most often use it with a time conjunction such as **when**, **after**, **as soon as**, and **by the time**:

*When I arrived he had already left.*
*After they'd shown their passports the guard let them in.*

**2** With certain verbs of intention; **hope**, **mean** and **intend**, the past perfect is used to express the fact that the intention did not happen.

*I had hoped to tell you earlier but it wasn't possible.*
*Apparently she'd meant to telephone you but her phone was out of order.*
*I'd intended to take the afternoon off but there was too much work to do.*

# PAST PERFECT PROGRESSIVE

## FORM

| | Pronoun/noun + auxiliary + present participle | | | |
|---|---|---|---|---|
| Affirmative | He | had been | working | a long time. |

The negative, interrogative and negative interrogative forms are formed in the same way as for the present perfect continuous but using **had been** instead of **have been**. See **Spotlight on Language p. 164**.

## USES

The past perfect progressive is used in the same way as the past perfect but the period of time indicated is longer, eg:

*The meeting had been going on for three hours by the time I arrived.*

**NB** The past perfect progressive passive exists but it is very rarely used. The following is an example just to show what it looks like.

*The escaped prisoner had been being looked for for ten years by the time the police found him.*

Now you know why we almost never use it!

# *Unit 7 Answers*

## EXERCISE 1

**1** I was living in Canterbury when Kennedy was assassinated.
**2** When I met her she was studying law.
**3** She fell aleep while he was reading.
**4** The road was being repaired when the accident happened.
**5** While we were eating the lights went out.

## EXERCISE 2

**1** Neither am I
**2** So do I
**3** Neither will I
**4** Neither can I
**5** So should I
**6** So might I
**7** So must I
**8** So did I
**9** So am I
**10** So will I

## EXERCISE 4

**1** Correct
**2** I enjoy playing tennis.
**3** He suggested going for a walk.
**4** Correct
**5** Do you mind helping me for a minute?
**6** Correct
**7** Before starting the meal please wash your hands.
**8** Your shirt needs ironing.
**9** Correct
**10** They missed seeing the film.

UNIT 8

# COUNTABLES AND UNCOUNTABLES

## FORMS

Countable nouns are nouns which we can count and they all have a plural form which is formed in the following ways:

1 By adding **-s** to the singular form:

*cat-cats*, *apple-apples*, *coat-coats* etc.

2 Nouns which end with **-y** preceded by a consonant drop the **-y** and add **-ies**:

*fly-flies*, *berry-berries*, *spy-spies* etc.

Nouns which end with a **-y** preceded by a vowel form plurals in the usual ways:

*boy-boys*, *toy-toys*, *way-ways* etc.

3 Nouns which end in **-ch**, **-sh**, **-ss**, and **-x** add **-es** for the plural:

*watch-watches*, *dish-dishes*, *class-classes*, *fox-foxes* etc.

4 Nouns ending in a consonant followed by **-o** add **-es**:

*tomato-tomatoes*, *potato-potatoes*, *hero-heroes* etc.

Nouns which end in **-o** preceded by a vowel add **-s**:

*radio-radios*

Similarly, nouns which end in **-o** but are abbreviations add **-s**:

*piano-pianos*, *photo-photos*, *micro-micros* etc.

5 Most nouns ending in **-f** or **-fe** drop the **-f** or **-fe** and add **-ves** for the plural:

*half-halves*, *knife-knives*, *leaf-leaves*, *life-lives*, *loaf-loaves*, *thief-thieves*, *wife-wives* etc.

6 Many other nouns have irregular plurals – the following ones are the most common:

*foot-feet*, *tooth-teeth*, *man-men*, *woman-women*

Uncountable nouns are nouns which we cannot count. They include most liquids, materials, and many things which we eat. They do not have a different plural form, they cannot be used with **a** or **an**, and they take a singular verb.

| **Liquids** | **Materials** | **Food** |
|---|---|---|
| water | gold | butter |
| blood | iron | sugar |
| milk | aluminium | spaghetti |
| whisky | wool | rice |
| wine | grass | bread |

There are some nouns that are countable in other languages but uncountable in English. The following are the most common ones:

| | | | |
|---|---|---|---|
| accommodation | hair | news | weather |
| advice | information | progress | work |
| baggage | knowledge | traffic | |
| furniture | luggage | trouble | |

## USES

The main difficulty is not deciding whether a noun is uncountable or not but remembering that different structures are used with a noun if it is countable or uncountable.

### **Much** and **many**

These are most often used in interrogative and negative sentences. **Much** is used when the noun is uncountable and **many** when the noun is countable:

*How much butter do we have?*
*They didn't have much information about the train crash.*
*How many players are there in a basketball team?*
*There weren't many spectators at the match.*

### **A little** and **a few**

**A little** is used with countables and **A few** with uncountables.

*There's a little bread left.*
*We have a few days left before we have to pay.*

**Such** and **so**

**Such** is used before an adjective followed by an uncountable noun to make the adjective stronger:

*It's such wonderful weather.*
*It's such good news.*

**Such a** is used before a countable noun with or without an adjective:

*It's such a lovely day.*
*I've got such a pain in my back.*

**So** is used before an adjective not followed immediately by a noun:

*He's so nice.*
*It's so cold in my flat.*

## NOUNS WHICH CAN BE COUNTABLE AND UNCOUNTABLE

Some nouns can be both countable and uncountable. They have different meanings depending on which way they are used. Look at these examples:

*I had three glasses of whisky before I went to bed.* Glass = container for liquid.

*Be careful! There's a lot of broken glass on the floor.* Glass = material.

*Don't sit in the back seat! There are a lot of dog hairs on it.* Individual hairs (countable).

*Many punks dye their hair different colours.* Hair on your head (uncountable).

**Exercise 1**

Look at these sentences and decide if they are correct. If they are not correct, write out the correct version.

**1** I can't eat all this. There is too much chips.
**2** I've heard such interesting informations.
**3** It's such a lovely evening – let's go for a swim.
**4** I have too few money to eat out tonight.
**5** We don't have many sugar left.
**6** She has very little luggage with her.
**7** This is such tasty an apple.
**8** He gave me a few chocolates.
**9** Many modern furniture is made of plastic.
**10** Don't eat too much pudding. You'll get fat!

## USED TO

### FORM

| | | | | | | |
|---|---|---|---|---|---|---|
| Affirmative | Pronoun/noun + used to + infinitive | | | | | |
| | I | used to | eat | meat. | | |
| Negative | Pronoun/noun + auxiliary + not + use to + infinitive | | | | | |
| | I | did | not | use to | eat | meat. |
| Interrogative | Auxiliary + pronoun/noun + use to + infinitive | | | | | |
| | Did | you | use to | eat | meat? | |
| Negative interrogative | Auxiliary + pronoun/noun + not + use to + infinitive | | | | | |
| | Did | you | not | use to | eat | meat? |
| Contraction | Didn't | you | | use to | eat | meat? |

**NB** It is also possible to say **usedn't** for the negative form but it is not common.

## USES

**Used to** is used to describe things which happened in the past but do not happen now. Usually it is used to express past habits. In the example above the speaker is expressing the fact that he used to eat meat but now he doesn't, perhaps for reasons of health. Compare these two sentences:

*I used to play tennis when I was young.*
*I played a lot of tennis last week.*

In the first sentence the speaker is indicating that he no longer plays tennis, in the second sentence the speaker is simply expressing a fact and it is very likely that he will continue to play tennis.

### would/wouldn't

*He would sit in the armchair in front of the fire every night.*
*The dog would go out hunting every night.*

This structure is sometimes used instead of 'used to' to describe past habits.
**NB** It cannot be used to describe past states:

*I used to live in Sweden* (**not** 'would').
*I would/used to ski to work in the winter.*

### Exercise 2

Look at the information about this person and make sentences using **used to**.

| | **Twenty years ago** | **Now** |
|---|---|---|
| WEIGHT | 70 kilos | 85 kilos |
| HAIR | Long | Short |
| GLASSES | No | Yes |
| BEARD | Yes | No |
| CLOTHES | Jeans | Suit |
| MUSIC | Jazz | Classical |
| TRANSPORT | Motorbike | Estate car |
| CIGARETTES | Yes | No |
| ALCOHOL | Yes | No |

# THE THIRD CONDITIONAL

## FORM

| | | | | | |
|---|---|---|---|---|---|
| | If + pronoun/noun + past perfect + pronoun/noun + perfect conditional | | | | |
| Affirmative | If | I | had known, | I | would have told you. |
| | If + pronoun/noun + past perfect + pronoun/noun + not + perf. cond. | | | | |
| Negative | If | I | had known, | I | wouldn't have told you. |
| | If + pronoun/noun + past perfect + perfect conditional | | | | |
| Interrogative | If | you | had known, | would you have told me? | |
| | If + pronoun/noun + past perfect + not + perfect conditional | | | | |
| Negative interrogative | If | you | had known, | would you not have told me? | |
| Contraction | If | you | had known, | wouldn't you have told me? | |

**NB** Like other conditional sentences (see **Spotlight on Language pp. 160 and 169**) the third conditional can be formed using either the conditional or the main clause first:

*If you had worked harder you would have passed your exams.*

*You'd have passed your exams if you'd worked harder.*

As third conditional sentences tend to be long, in speech we often contract them:

| In formal writing | In informal writing | In speech |
|---|---|---|
| I would have<br>I would not have | I would've or I'd have<br>I wouldn't have | I'd've<br>I wouldn't've |

## FUNCTION

The third conditional is often called the impossible or the unreal conditional because it refers to events which did not happen in the past. Because third conditional sentences are long, in speech we often use only the first part of the sentence when reacting to someone's statement:

A: *I've got stomach ache.*
B: *Well; if you hadn't eaten so many sweets* . . . (you wouldn't have stomach ache)

A: *My boss shouted at me.*
B: *Ah! But if you hadn't been late* . . . (he wouldn't have shouted at you)

**Exercise 3**

Look at the following pairs of statements and make a third conditional sentence out of them. An example has been done for you:

| | |
|---|---|
| Go on holiday | enough money |

*I would have gone on holiday if I'd had enough money.*

| | | |
|---|---|---|
| **1** | I missed my bus | I got up late |
| **2** | He was sent to prison | he stole a car |
| **3** | She wanted to speak to me | my telephone wasn't working |
| **4** | He won a gold medal | he took drugs |
| **5** | They drowned | they couldn't swim |

# *Unit 8 Answers*

## EXERCISE 1

**1** I can't eat all this. There are too many chips.
**2** I've heard such interesting information.
**3** Correct
**4** I have too little money to eat out tonight.
**5** We don't have much sugar left.
**6** Correct
**7** This is such a tasty apple.
**8** Correct
**9** Much modern furniture is made of plastic.
**10** Correct

## EXERCISE 2

A variety of answers can be made using the information supplied. The following are some examples:
He used to weigh 70 kilos.
He used to have long hair.
He didn't use to wear glasses.
He used to have a beard.
He used to wear jeans.
He used to like Jazz.
He used to ride a motorbike.
He used to smoke.
He used to drink alcohol.

## EXERCISE 3

**1** I wouldn't have missed my bus if I hadn't got up late.
**2** He wouldn't have been sent to prison if he hadn't stolen a car.
**3** She would have been able to speak to me if my telephone had been working.
**4** He wouldn't have won a gold medal if he hadn't taken drugs.
**5** They wouldn't have drowned if they had been able to swim.

UNIT
9

# THE IMPERATIVE

## FORM

| | |
|---|---|
| Affirmative | Infinitive without to |
| | Sit down. |
| Negative | Auxiliary (do) + not + infinitive without to |
| | Do not (Don't) shout. |

The imperative is usually used without a noun or pronoun but to make it clear who we are talking to we can put the noun or pronoun before or after the imperative. Look at these examples:

*Christine, shut up.*
*Nobody leave the room.*
*Throw it over here, Martin.*

The imperative form of **do** or **be** is used to give more emphasis to the statement. **Do** is followed by a verb and **Be** is followed by an adjective:

*Do take a seat.*
*Don't tell me.*

*Do be sensible.*
*Don't be sad.*

## USES

### Commands and orders

To tell somebody either to do something or not do something we often use the imperative. Often the imperative is used by somebody who is in authority, a parent, a teacher, an officer in the army, etc:

*Sit down.*
*Don't touch that.*

### Advice

The imperative is also used for giving advice. Look at these examples:

*'I've got a headache.' 'Take an aspirin.'*
*'I'm very tired.' 'Lie down for an hour or two.'*

### Directions and instructions

When we give instructions in speech or writing we often use the imperative:

*Go straight ahead and turn left at the traffic lights.*
*Beat an egg with salt and pepper then add half a cup of flour and mix until smooth.*

# VERBS TAKING THE INFINITIVE AND/OR THE GERUND

When a verb is followed by another verb, the first verb usually expresses our opinion about the action described by the second verb. Some verbs are followed by the infinitive, others by the gerund. A few verbs can be followed by either the infinitive or the gerund but the meaning is usually different depending on which form they are followed by.

### Verb + infinitive

The most common verbs which only take the infinitive are as follows:

| | | | | | | |
|---|---|---|---|---|---|---|
| afford | ask | decide | happen | manage | promise | want |
| agree | beg | determine | help | mean | refuse | wish |
| appear | choose | expect | hope | offer | seem | |
| arrange | dare | fail | learn | prepare | tend | |

### Verb + gerund

The most common verbs which only take the gerund are as follows.

| | | | | | |
|---|---|---|---|---|---|
| admit | consider | enjoy | finish | mention | practise |
| appreciate | delay | escape | forgive | mind | suggest |
| avoid | deny | feel | imagine | miss | understand |

### Verb + infinitive or gerund

Some verbs can take either the gerund or infinitive.

**1 Verbs expressing feelings:**

*can't bear, dislike, hate, like, love*

**Can't bear** has a similar meaning when followed by a gerund or infinitive.

*I can't bear seeing children smoking. =*
*I can't bear to see children smoking.*

**Like** can be used to mean **enjoy** or **It is a good idea to**. When it is used as **enjoy**, **like** is followed by a gerund.

*I like swimming.*

When it is used as **It is a good idea to** it is followed by an infinitive.

*I like to do my homework before going home.*

When we use **would** with **like**, **dislike**, **love** and **hate** the following verb takes the infinitive form.

*I'd like to learn the piano.*
*I'd hate to be out of work.*

**2 Verbs expressing stages of an action**

*begin, start, continue, stop*

Usually these verbs can be followed by either the gerund or infinitive.

*I began to learn French when I was seven. = I began learning French when I was seven.*

However **stop** has a different meaning depending on whether it is followed by a gerund or infinitive.

*I stopped seeing him because he was so rude.*

This means that you decided not to see him again.

*I stopped to see him on my way home.*

This means I interrupted my journey home in order to see him.

**3 Remember**

When **remember** = remembered something before doing it, **remember** is followed by the infinitive.

*I remembered to cancel the newspapers before going on holiday.*

When **remember** = remember having done something, **remember** is followed by the gerund.

*I remember hating school when I was young.*

### Exercise 1

Look at these sentences containing verbs which take the infinitive or gerund. Decide which ones are incorrect and write down the correct version.

1 I look forward to meet you.
2 I'm afraid to go out alone.
3 Do you remember meeting her.
4 He really enjoys to go swimming.
5 My father didn't allow me drinking.
6 They let me attend the wedding.
7 I stopped to eat meat when I was twenty.
8 I can't help to be fat.
9 She decided against to go to the theatre.
10 I'm glad I've finished to do my homework.

# *Unit 9 Answers*

## EXERCISE 1

1 I look forward to meeting you.
2 Correct *or* I am afraid of going out alone.
3 Correct.
4 He really enjoys going swimming.
5 My father didn't allow me to drink.
6 Correct.
7 I stopped eating meat when I was twenty.
8 I can't help being fat.
9 She decided against going to the theatre.
10 I'm glad I've finished doing my homework.

UNIT 10

# INDIRECT SPEECH (1)

When we report what somebody has said we either use direct speech using the speaker's exact words or indirect speech where we try to convey the speaker's intentions without quoting the actual words used. Direct speech is most often used in literary works such as novels; indirect speech is more often used to report something in speech or writing. Look at this example:

John's actual words: 'I'm very tired.'
Direct speech: 'I'm very tired,' said John.
Indirect speech: John said he was very tired.

In indirect speech the tense of the verb changed from the present simple to the past simple. This is because John's utterance took place earlier than the person's who reported it. In general, in indirect speech the tense used for the reporting moves one back from the tense the speaker used. Look at the following table:

| **Direct speech** | **Indirect speech** |
|---|---|
| **Present simple**<br>'I love classical music.' | **Past simple**<br>He said he loved classical music. |
| **Present progressive**<br>'I'm having a shower.' | **Past progressive**<br>He said he was having a shower. |
| **Past simple**<br>'I enjoyed the meal.' | **Past perfect**<br>He said he had enjoyed the meal. |
| **Present perfect**<br>'I've read the newspapers.' | **Past perfect**<br>He said he had read the newspapers. |
| **Present perfect progressive**<br>'I've been watching television.' | **Past perfect progressive**<br>He said he had been watching television. |
| **Past progressive**<br>'I was working late.' | **Past perfect progressive**<br>He said he had been working late. |
| **Past perfect**<br>'I'd never been there before.' | **Past perfect**<br>He said he had never been there before. |
| **Shall/will**<br>'I'll see Jane later.' | **Should/would**<br>He said he would see Jane later. |
| **Can/may**<br>'I can smell burning.'<br>'I may come.' | **Could/might**<br>He said he could smell burning.<br>He said he might come. |

**Could**, **might**, **must**, **ought**, **should**, and **would**, no change.

| | |
|---|---|
| 'I must do my homework.' | *He said he had to do his homework. |
| 'I would love to go to Rome.' | He said he would love to go to Rome. |

* When we turn a sentence with **must** in it into reported speech it is also possible to use **must**.

*'I must catch my train.'* — *He said he must catch his train.*

**Shall** and **should** often change to **would** in indirect speech because of the different pronoun.

*'I should love to meet you.'* — *He said he would love to meet me.*

### Other changes in indirect speech

In addition to the changes in pronouns and tenses that we have looked at, there are other changes to make to the speaker's actual words. These changes nearly always refer to time or place:

| | |
|---|---|
| *here* | *there* |
| *now* | *then* |
| *tomorrow* | *the next day* |
| *yesterday* | *the previous day* |
| *this* | *that* |
| *now* | *then* |
| *last* | *the previous* |
| *next* | *the following* |

## SAY AND TELL

**Say** and **tell** are both used in indirect speech to report statements and information. They are never used to report questions. In indirect speech **tell** is always followed by a direct object, ie the person the information was given to. **Say** is not followed by a direct object.

| | |
|---|---|
| Mary's actual words: | *'It's eight o'clock.'* |
| Reported with **say**: | *She said it was eight o'clock.* |
| Reported with **tell**: | *She told me it was eight o'clock.* |

Both **say** and **tell** can be followed by **that**.

| | |
|---|---|
| Mary's actual words: | *I'm eating out tonight.* |
| Reported with **say**: | *She said that she was eating out that night.* |
| or: | *She said to John that she was eating out that night.* |
| Reported with **tell**: | *She told John that she was eating out that night.* |

### Exercise 1

Put the following into indirect speech making any changes that are necessary to tenses, pronouns, and expressions of time and place.

1. 'John, you didn't clean the bath,' she said.
2. 'I wouldn't like to live here,' she said.
3. 'My holidays start next week,' she told me.
4. 'I must go now,' she said.
5. 'We'll telephone Jane's mother tomorrow,' she said.
6. 'I hadn't realised you were married,' she said.
7. 'I haven't seen him since last Thursday,' she said.
8. 'I think it may rain,' she said.
9. 'I hope you are not angry,' she said.
10. 'I was washing the car when you phoned,' she told him.

## DEFINING CLAUSES

Defining clauses are used to identify the person or object that you are speaking about. Without a defining clause the statement would make little sense. Look at these examples:

*I saw the woman (who bought your old flat) this morning.*
*Can you pass me the book (which is on the mantlepiece)?*

Without the defining clause we would not know which woman or book the speaker was referring to.

### Defining clauses with relative pronouns

**Who**, **which**, **where** and **whose** are often used in defining clauses. Note that **who** is used for a person, **which** for a thing and **where** for a place. Here are a few examples:

*I don't like the man who is talking to Mandy.*
*I've bought the car which was advertised in yesterday's paper.*
*Do you know the couple whose house burnt down?*
*I went to the town where we saw the bullfight.*

### Defining clauses with that

**That** is used instead of relative pronouns after certain words and expressions such as **all**, **anything**, **everything**, **few**, **little**, **much**, **none**, **nothing**, **no-one**, **only**:

*Have we got all (that) we need?*
*Is there anything (that) I can bring you?*
*She has everything (that) she needs.*

In speech, **that** can be omitted altogether.

### Exercise 2

In this exercise make one sentence out of the two sentences given. Look first at the example:

I like the car. The car is in the window.
*I like the car which is in the window.*

1. He telephoned the woman. The woman was holding a party.
2. They are the couple. Their picture was in the newspaper.
3. The prize was won by the dog. The dog was wearing a tartan collar.
4. He ate the sandwiches. There were a few sandwiches left.
5. Take the umbrella. The umbrella is in the hall.
6. We must go back to the restaurant. You left your bag there.

# *Unit 10 Answers*

## EXERCISE 1

**1** She told John that he hadn't cleaned the bath.
**2** She said that she wouldn't like to live there.
**3** She said that her holidays started the following week.
**4** She said that she had to/must go then.
**5** She said that they would telephone Jane's mother the following day.
**6** She said that she hadn't realised that he was married.
**7** She said that she hadn't seen him since the previous Thursday.
**8** She said she thought it might rain.
**9** She said that she hoped he wasn't angry.
**10** She said that she was washing the car when he phoned.

## EXERCISE 2

**1** He telephoned the woman who was holding a party.
**2** They are the couple whose picture was in the newspaper.
**3** The prize was won by the dog which was wearing the tartan collar.
**4** He ate the few sandwiches which were left.
**5** Take the umbrella which is in the hall.
**6** We must go back to the restaurant where you left your bag.

UNIT 11

## NON-DEFINING CLAUSES

In **Spotlight on Language p. 182** we saw that defining clauses were necessary to identify clearly the person or object that we were speaking about. Non-defining clauses are not needed to identify the person we are speaking about, but simply provide extra information. They are not used very much in spoken English and are more frequent in writing:

| | |
|---|---|
| Defining: | *He's borrowed the book which my mother gave me.* |
| Non-defining: | *He's borrowed 'Animal Farm', which was written by George Orwell.* |
| Defining: | *I gave him the wine which I bought in Yugoslavia.* |
| Non-defining: | *I gave him a bottle of wine, which he immediately dropped.* |

Note also that non-defining clauses are separated from their noun by a comma. If the sentence goes on after the clause it is again separated by a comma.

**Exercise 1**

Join the two sentences to make one longer sentence. The non-defining clause is sometimes at the end of the longer sentence or sometimes in the middle.

**1** Shakespeare was born in Stratford-upon-Avon. He was a playwright.
**2** I saw Bob Nicholson this morning. His wife is on holiday.
**3** They ate at the Savoy. It is the most famous hotel in London.
**4** My cousin is coming to stay. He has a farm in Scotland.
**5** I saw 'Casablanca' last night. It is my favourite film.

## FUTURE TIME CLAUSES

Time conjunctions such as **after**, **as soon as**, **before**, **until**, **when**, **whenever**, and the conjunctions **whatever**, **whoever** and **no matter what** are not normally followed by the **will** form, but by a present tense. Look at these examples:

*We'll eat after he goes.*
*As soon as we finish work we'll go for a swim.*
*I'm afraid I won't be able to see you before you go.*
*The strike will continue until the management raises the wages.*

**Exercise 2**

Each of the following sentences contains a tense mistake. Write down the correct form.

**1** He'll give me back the money as soon as he will be paid.
**2** I won't tell her before I'll know.
**3** I'd leave before I would be sacked.
**4** No matter what will happen, I'll telephone tomorrow.
**5** After I'll arrive we'll have lunch.

# *Unit 11 Answers*

## EXERCISE 1

**1** Shakespeare, the playwright, was born in Stratford-upon-Avon.
**2** I saw Bob Nicholson, whose wife is on holiday, this morning.
**3** They ate at the Savoy, the most famous hotel in London.
**4** My cousin, who has a farm in Scotland, is coming to stay.
**5** I saw 'Casablanca', my favourite film, last night.

## EXERCISE 2

**1** He'll give me back the money as soon as he is paid.
**2** I won't tell her before I know.
**3** I'd leave before I was sacked.
**4** No matter what happens, I'll telephone tomorrow.
**5** After I arrive we'll have lunch.

# FUTURE PROGRESSIVE ACTIVE

## FORM

| | | | | | | |
|---|---|---|---|---|---|---|
| Affirmative | Pronoun/noun + will/shall + be + present participle | | | | | |
| | I | shall | | be | seeing | him later. |
| Negative | Pronoun/noun + will/shall + not + be + present participle | | | | | |
| | I | shall | not | be | seeing | him later. |
| Interrogative | Will/shall + pronoun/noun + be + present participle | | | | | |
| | Will | you | | be | seeing | him later? |
| Negative interrogative | Will/shall + pronoun/noun + not + be + present participle | | | | | |
| | Will | you | not | be | seeing | him later? |
| Contraction | Won't | you | | be | seeing | him later? |

Remember that **shall** and **will** contract to **'ll**, that **shall not** contracts to **shan't** and **will not** contracts to **won't**.

# FUTURE PROGRESSIVE PASSIVE

This form is very rarely used in either speech or writing.

# FUTURE PROGRESSIVE ACTIVE

## USE

The future progressive is used to describe an action that will be taking place at some specified point in the future, and which has already been decided.

*Next week I'll be working in London.*
*Please don't come round tomorrow. I'll be painting the flat.*

When it is used in the interrogative it is often used as a polite method of asking about somebody's future arrangements.

*Will you be taking your holiday next week?*
*Will you be needing me to work late this week?*

TO HAVE/GET SOMETHING DONE

These constructions are sometimes called the 'phoney passive' because it indicates that the required action is not to be carried out by the speaker. Look at these examples:

*I'm going to have my hair cut.*
(The hairdresser will cut it.)
*I used to have/get my eyes tested.*
(The optician will test them.)
*I must have my suit cleaned.*
(The Dry Cleaner's will clean it.)

# THE FUTURE PERFECT ACTIVE

## FORM

| | |
|---|---|
| Affirmative | Pronoun/noun + will/shall have + past participle |
| | You will have finished your work by tonight. |
| Negative | Pronoun/noun + won't/shan't have + past participle |
| | You won't have finished your work by tonight. |
| Interrogative | Will/shall + pronoun/noun + have + past participle |
| | Will you have finished your work by tonight? |
| Negative interrogative | Will/shall + pronoun/noun + not + have + past participle |
| | Will you not have finished your work by tonight? |
| Contraction | Won't you have finished your work by tonight? |

**NB** There is also a future perfect progressive form:

*I will have been going out with him for six months by next Thursday.*

but it is rarely used.

The passive form of the future perfect is also not used very frequently but the following are examples:

*The contracts will have been signed by Monday.*
*The repairs will have been done by next month.*

## USE

The future perfect is used to describe an action that will have been completed by a certain time in the future. The future perfect is nearly always followed by **by**.

**Exercise 1**

Look at these sentences and decide which ones are correct. Rewrite the incorrect ones using an appropriate future form.

**1** The film finishes at 11 o'clock.
**2** I am staying here until he will come.
**3** I'll have lived here 10 years by next month.
**4** I expect he'll arrive there by now.
**5** Watch out! That icicle will fall.
**6** The World Cup starts next week.
**7** He thinks I'm passing my exam next month.
**8** They'll be arriving shortly.
**9** I think it's snowing tomorrow.
**10** How long will you have to stay there?

# INDIRECT SPEECH (2) REPORTING QUESTIONS

**Spotlight on Language p. 181** showed how to report statements and the changes in pronouns, tenses and other aspects to be made in reported speech. There are two ways to turn questions into indirect speech depending on the type of question.

### Questions beginning with a question word

Questions that begin with a question word such as **how**, **who**, **where**, **when** etc. have a different word order when reported in indirect speech and do not include the auxiliary **do**. Look at these examples.

| **Actual question** | **Question in indirect speech** |
|---|---|
| *'Who is that man?'* | *He asked me who that man was.* |
| *'How far is it to London?'* | *He asked me how far it was to London.* |
| *'Where did you go to school?'* | *He asked me where I'd been to school.* |
| *'What time is it?'* | *He asked me what time it was.* |
| *'When did you arrive?'* | *He asked me what time I arrived.* |
| *'Why are you looking angry?'* | *He asked me why I was looking angry.* |

The word order of the pronoun and verb is reversed in indirect speech and is the same word order as for an affirmative statement. In addition to not using the auxiliary **do**, a question mark is not used for a reported question.

**Questions that do not begin with a question word**

Questions that do not begin with a question word use **if** or **whether** when turned into indirect speech. Usually it does not matter whether **if** or **whether** is used, eg:

Actual question: 'Do you want tea or coffee?'
Indirect speech: He asked whether I wanted tea or coffee.

| **Actual question** | **Question in indirect speech** |
|---|---|
| *'Have you been here before?'* | *He asked me if/whether I had been there before.* |
| *'Would you like a coffee?'* | *He asked me if/whether I would like a coffee.* |
| *'Are you coming this afternoon?'* | *He asked me if/whether I was coming that afternoon.* |
| *'Have you been studying long?'* | *He asked me if/whether I had been studying long.* |
| *'Could you give me a hand?'* | *He asked me if/whether I could give him a hand.* |

**Exercise 2**

Turn the following questions into indirect questions.

**1** 'What time did you arrive?'
**2** 'How long did the journey take?'
**3** 'Was the train on time?'
**4** 'Have you already eaten?'
**5** 'Is it the first time you have been to London?'
**6** 'Where will you be staying?'
**7** 'How much are they charging you?'
**8** 'Would you like to go sightseeing?'
**9** 'Do you prefer art galleries or museums?'
**10** 'Shall we take a taxi?'

# *Unit 12 Answers*

## EXERCISE 1

**1** Correct
**2** I am staying here until he comes.
**3** Correct
**4** I expect he'll have arrived there by now.
**5** Watch out! That icicle is going to fall.
**6** Correct
**7** He thinks I'll pass my exam next month.
**8** Correct
**9** I think it will snow tomorrow.
**10** Correct

## EXERCISE 2

**1** He asked me what time I had arrived.
**2** He asked me how long the journey had taken.
**3** He asked me if the train was on time/had been on time.
**4** He asked me if I had already eaten.
**5** He asked me if that was the first time I had been in London.
**6** He asked me where I would be staying.
**7** He asked me how much they were charging me.
**8** He asked me if I would like to go sightseeing.
**9** He asked me if I preferred art galleries or museums.
**10** He asked me if we should take a taxi.

## MODALS (2) PAST DEDUCTION

Modals of deduction have been discussed in **Spotlight on Language p. 166**. **Can't**, **must**, **need**, **might**, and **could** can also be used to express past deduction or to express a conclusion based on evidence that we have.

### Can't have/couldn't have

*It can't have been him at the party.*

We might say this because we now know for definite that he wasn't in the area at the time of the party.

*He couldn't have killed her.*

We might say this because we know for a fact that he was somewhere else when she was killed.

### May have/might have

*He may have telephoned.*

We are not sure because nobody was by the phone all the time.

*He might have telephoned.*

This sentence has two meanings depending how it is said. If **might** is stressed then it has the same meaning as the sentence above for **may** (possibility). If **telephoned** is stressed then we are expressing disappointment or anger because we know he didn't telephone, and wanted him to.

### Needn't have

*You needn't have bought me a present.*

This expresses the fact that it was not necessary for your friend to buy you a present but that he or she did, anyway.

### Must have

*He must have gone out.*

This expresses a logical conclusion because, for example, there are no lights on in his house.

## INDIRECT SPEECH (3) REPORTING VERBS

Reported statements using **say** and **tell** are discussed in **Spotlight on Language p. 182** and reported questions in **Spotlight on Language p. 186**. People also convey their emotions by the language that they use and the tone of voice they adopt. They can indicate that they are angry, sympathetic, worried, nervous and many other things. To simply use **say**, **tell**, and **ask** does not relate accurately what they intended to convey; a wide range of other verbs is used to report what they have said. The most common ones are as follows:

### Advise

This is often used to report advice that somebody has given and it is followed by **to**.

| | |
|---|---|
| *'You should see a doctor.'* | *She advised me to see a doctor.* |
| *'Take an aspirin.'* | *He advised her to take an aspirin.* |

### Suggest

This is also used like **advise** to report advice but it is also used to report suggestions. It is followed by **that** or by the gerund.

| | |
|---|---|
| *'Take an aspirin.'* | *She suggested that I took an aspirin.*<br>or<br>*She suggested taking an aspirin.* |
| *'How about going to the cinema?'* | *He suggested that we went to the cinema.*<br>or<br>*He suggested going to the cinema.* |

Although both forms are correct, we usually use **that** when we want to make it clear who the suggestion was made to.

### Apologise

This is used to report apologies, most commonly when the statement includes the phrases **I'm sorry** or **I'm afraid**. **Apologise** is followed by **for** and the gerund.

| | |
|---|---|
| *'I'm sorry I'm late.'* | *He apologised for being late.* |
| *'I'm afraid I can't come.'* | *He apologised for not being able to come.* |

### Invite

This is used to report invitations and is usually followed by **to** or **for**.

| | |
|---|---|
| *'Would you like to come for a drink?'* | *He invited me to come for a drink.* |
| *'Please come and have tea with me.'* | *She invited me for tea.* |

### Warn

This is used to report warnings. In the affirmative it is followed by **that** and in the negative by **not to**.

| | |
|---|---|
| *'The police are coming.'* | *He warned me that the police were coming.* |
| *'Don't drink the water.'* | *He warned me not to drink the water.* |

### Remind

This is used to report reminders and is followed by **to** or a clause beginning with **it** or **that**.

| | |
|---|---|
| *'Don't forget to turn off the lights.'* | *He reminded me to turn off the lights.* |
| *'Remember it's our wedding anniversary next week.'* | *He reminded me it was our wedding anniversary the following week.* |

### Offer

This is used to report offers and is followed by **to** or an object.

| | |
|---|---|
| *'I'll give you a lift.'* | *He offered to give me a lift.* |
| *'Have a cup of tea.'* | *He offered me a cup of tea.* |

### Deny

This is used to report denials and is followed by **that** or by the gerund.

| | |
|---|---|
| *'I didn't steal the car.'* | *He denied stealing the car.*<br>or<br>*He denied that he had stolen the car.* |
| *'It's not my fault.'* | *He denied that it was his fault.* |

### Other reporting verbs

There are other reporting verbs in English but they are not so common. Here are a few examples:

| | |
|---|---|
| Beg: *'Please, please don't leave me.'* | *He begged me not to leave him.* |
| Recommend: *'Lose weight!'* | *He recommended that I lost weight.* |
| Order: *'Be quiet!'* | *He ordered me to be quiet.* |

### Exercise 2

Turn the following expressions into indirect speech using an appropriate reporting verb; do not use **say** or **tell**.

**1** 'Don't play with matches.'
**2** 'Buy the new Stones LP. It's great.'
**3** 'Let me carry your case.'
**4** 'Come and stay next weekend.'
**5** 'It wasn't me who broke the window.'
**6** 'I'm afraid I have spilt my wine on the carpet.'
**7** 'Let's leave now.'
**8** 'Remember, shops shut early today.'
**9** 'Try to get more sleep.'
**10** 'Get out of my office.'

# *Unit 13 Answers*

## EXERCISE 1

**1** He warned me not to play with matches.
**2** He suggested that I bought the new Stones LP.
**3** He offered to carry my case.
**4** He invited me to come and stay the following weekend.
**5** He denied breaking the window.
**6** He apologised for spilling the wine on the carpet.
**7** He suggested leaving then.
**8** He reminded me that shops shut early that day.
**9** He advised me to get more sleep.
**10** He ordered me out of his office.

# *Irregular Verbs*

This is a list of some of the most common irregular verbs.

| Infinitive | Past tense | Past participle | Infinitive | Past tense | Past participle |
|---|---|---|---|---|---|
| be | was | been | let | let | let |
| become | became | became | lie | lay | lain |
| beat | beat | beaten | lose | lost | lost |
| begin | began | begun | make | made | made |
| bend | bent | bent | mean | meant | meant |
| bet | bet | bet | meet | met | met |
| bid | bid | bid | pay | paid | paid |
| bite | bit | bitten | put | put | put |
| bleed | bled | bled | read | read | read |
| blow | blew | blown | ride | rode | ridden |
| break | broke | broken | ring | rang | rung |
| bring | brought | brought | rise | rose | risen |
| build | built | built | run | ran | run |
| burn | burned/t | burned/t | say | said | said |
| buy | bought | bought | see | saw | seen |
| catch | caught | caught | sell | sold | sold |
| choose | chose | chosen | send | sent | sent |
| come | came | come | set | set | set |
| creep | crept | crept | shake | shook | shaken |
| cost | cost | cost | shine | shone | shone |
| cut | cut | cut | shoot | shot | shot |
| deal | dealt | dealt | show | showed | shown |
| dig | dug | dug | shut | shut | shut |
| do | did | done | sing | sang | sung |
| draw | drew | drawn | sink | sank | sunk |
| dream | dreamt | dreamt | sit | sat | sat |
| drink | drank | drunk | sleep | slept | slept |
| drive | drove | driven | slide | slid | slid |
| eat | ate | eaten | sing | sang | sung |
| fall | fell | fallen | smell | smelt | smelt |
| feed | fed | fed | speak | spoke | spoken |
| feel | felt | felt | speed | sped | sped |
| fight | fought | fought | spill | spilt | spilt |
| find | found | found | spend | spent | spent |
| flee | fled | fled | spit | spat | spat |
| fly | flew | flown | spread | spread | spread |
| forget | forgot | forgotten | stand | stood | stood |
| freeze | froze | frozen | steal | stole | stolen |
| get | got | got | stick | stuck | stuck |
| give | gave | given | strike | struck | struck |
| go | went | gone | swear | swore | sworn |
| grow | grew | grown | sweep | swept | swept |
| hang | hung | hung | swim | swam | swum |
| *for people* | hanged | hanged | swing | swung | swung |
| hear | heard | heard | take | took | taken |
| hide | hid | hidden | teach | taught | taught |
| hit | hit | hit | tear | tore | torn |
| hold | held | held | tell | told | told |
| hurt | hurt | hurt | think | thought | thought |
| keep | kept | kept | throw | threw | thrown |
| know | knew | known | understand | understood | understood |
| lay | laid | laid | wake | woke | woken |
| lead | led | led | wear | wore | worn |
| lean | leant | leant | win | won | won |
| learn | learned/t | learned/t | wind | wound | wound |
| leave | left | left | write | wrote | written |
| lend | lent | lent | | | |